T0128975

Solving Management's Puzzle

The Art of Managing People and Adapting in An Overseas Environment

DAVID KORPONAI

Order this book online at www.trafford.com
or email orders@trafford.com

Most Trafford titles are also available at major online book retailers.

Initial formatting and layout by Momcilo Vuckovic

© Copyright 2012 David Korponai.
All rights reserved. No part of this publication may be reproduced, stored in a retrieval
system, or transmitted, in any form or by any means, electronic, mechanical, photocopying,
recording, or otherwise, without the written prior permission of the author.

Printed in the United States of America.

ISBN: 978-1-4669-0164-3 (sc)
ISBN: 978-1-4669-0165-0 (e)

Trafford rev. 06/25/2012

 www.trafford.com

North America & international
toll-free: 1 888 232 4444 (USA & Canada)
phone: 250 383 6864 ♦ fax: 812 355 4082

CONTENTS

DEDICATION

WHILE A DEDICATION did not cross my mind at first I was moved by a tribute paid to Jasper Howard a University of Connecticut football player whose life was tragically cut short when he was fatally stabbed while attending a sanctioned school dance at the university Student Union on October 17, 2009. I saw this after being coaxed to visit the UConn campus by a dear friend of mine in September 2010.

Jasper is quoted as saying:

"You have to play each play like it's the last play you'll ever play."

To paraphrase this:

"You have to live every day like it's the last day you'll ever live."

So goes it with those who serve in harm's way or serve or live in countries where conditions may be far outside of their comfort zone.

COVER TRANSLATIONS

1. Spanish: *Una forma unica y detallada de gerenciar y adaptarce en mercados internacionales.*

    Translation: **An in-depth, unique look at managing and adapting in an overseas environment.**

2. Russian: *Обязательное чтение для менеджера, работающего в зарубежном государстве.*

    Translation: **A must read for the overseas manager.**

3. German: *Kein Unsinn-Konzept zur Verwaltung in einem fremden Land.*

    Translation: **No Nonsense approach to managing in a foreign country.**

DISCLAIMER

AS A PERSONAL Services Contract employee of a United States Government agency, I would like to make one point perfectly clear. I am reasonably assured that there is nothing in this printed text that is of an official concern. Therefore, this text is not subject to any clearance procedures and is in compliance with 3 FAM 4170.

All opinions and views expressed herein are those of the Author and not necessarily those of the United States Agency for International Development or any other U.S. Government agency.

—◆—

OPENING

WITH NUMEROUS TRADE agreements in place, or in the works it seems inevitable that expansion abroad should be on the corporate agenda. This is true of not only manufacturing operations but expanding markets as well. To do this various elements of a company's work force *must* become even more mobile than they are now. However, expansion abroad does not necessarily mean the loss of jobs. The potential for economic growth and job creation within the home country, a la main land China needs to be factored into the overseas expansion equation. If you want to get a better idea of the international trade agreements that I am talking about just Google it. To save you some time, the following list of current and proposed international free trade agreements was recently extracted from *Google*:

Operating agreements

- Asia-Pacific Trade Agreement (APTA)—31 July 1975[1]—renamed 2 November 2005[2]

- ASEAN Free Trade Area (AFTA)

  - ASEAN—China
  - ASEAN—India

- African Free Trade Zone (AFTZ)

  - East African Community (EAC)
  - Common Market for Eastern and Southern Africa (COMESA)

- ○ Southern African Development Community (SADC)
  - ▪ Southern African Customs Union (SACU)

- Caribbean Community (CARICOM)

- Central European Free Trade Agreement (CEFTA)

- Closer Economic Partnership Arrangement (CEPA)

- Dominican Republic—Central America Free Trade Agreement (DR-CAFTA)—5 August 2004[3]

  - ○ Central American Integration System (SICA)

- Economic Community of Central African States (ECCAS)

  - ○ Economic and Monetary Community of Central Africa (CEMAC)

- Economic Community of West African States (ECOWAS)

  - ○ West African Economic and Monetary Union (UEMOA)
  - ○ West African Monetary Zone (WAMZ)

- European Economic Area (EEA)

  - ○ European Free Trade Association (EFTA)

- Commonwealth of Independent States Free Trade Agreement (CISFTA)—15 April 1994[4]

  - ○ Eurasian Economic Community (EAEC)—29 March 1996[5]

- Greater Arab Free Trade Area (GAFTA)—June 1957[6]

  - ○ Gulf Cooperation Council (GCC)

- Intergovernmental Authority on Development (IGAD)

- Latin American Integration Association (ALADI)—18 February 1960[7]

  ◦ Andean Community (CAN)
  ◦ G-3 Free Trade Agreement (G-3)
  ◦ Mercosur (Mercosul)

- Trans-Pacific Strategic Economic Partnership (TPP)

- North American Free Trade Agreement (NAFTA)

- Pacific Island Countries Trade Agreement (PICTA)

- South Asia Free Trade Agreement (SAFTA)

Proposed agreements

- Arab Maghreb Union (UMA)

- Asia-Pacific Economic Cooperation (APEC)

- Association of Caribbean States (ACS)

- Bolivarian Alternative for the Americas (ALBA)

- Bay of Bengal Initiative for MultiSectoral Technical and Economic Cooperation (BIMSTEC)

- Canada Central American Free Trade Agreement

- Community of Sahel-Saharan States (CEN-SAD)

- Comprehensive Economic Partnership for East Asia (CEPEA)

- European Union Central American Association Agreement (EU-CAAA)

- European Union Economic Partnership Agreement with the Pacific ACP Countries (EU-PACP)

- Euro-Mediterranean free trade area (EU-MEFTA)

- Free Trade Area of the Americas (FTAA)

- Free Trade Area of the Asia Pacific (FTAAP)

- GUAM Organization for Democracy and Economic Development (GUAM)[8]

- Intergovernmental Authority on Development (IGAD)

- Middle East Free Trade Area (US-MEFTA)

- North American Union (NAU)

- People's Trade Treaty of Bolivarian Alternative for the Americas (ALBA)

- Shanghai Cooperation Organization (SCO)[9]

- Transatlantic Free Trade Area (TAFTA)

- Trust Territory of the Pacific Islands (TTPI)

- Union of South American Nations (CSN)

Faster means of transportation and communications are not only making our world a smaller place to live in, but they are opening up markets at a breathtaking pace. While markets are expanding, competition for market share is getting stronger and more competitive than ever. Let's face it; we have had a complex global economy for a long time. In my opinion international companies can target various regions while still tailoring marketing strategies to individual country clients.

In some cases, cut-throat tactics and bribery are common place. How will your company react when these circumstance arise?

More important, how will you the more effective manager react and what can you do to *better adjust* in a foreign country that, in many instances will be thousands of miles away from your headquarters and possibly, from your family and friends as well. In accepting a position overseas you may be moving out of your comfort zone.

CHAPTER I

—═◆═—

INTRODUCTION

FOR THOSE OF you who may not have read my first book, **Solving Management's Puzzle—The Art of Managing People** let me say that the 56 elements (See Appendix A) that a more effective manager should be aware of and that were identified and discussed in that book are also applicable in an overseas environment. In addition to those, the 50 awareness components discussed here are overseas specific and slanted towards managing and adapting in that environment. They deserve special attention.

As you will soon find out once you become aware of these components they will help you build a solid foundation that you can use to become a more effective manager. Managing is not that difficult. However, the overseas working environment presents us with additional challenges that we should be aware of: hence, the reason for and theme for this book.

The degree that you should be aware of these will vary from country to country. In rare cases something discussed may not be relevant to your need. For example, the discussion about language may not be applicable to an American assigned to or working in England. Other awareness elements will be of interest however. The knowledge and understanding that you gain after reading this book will make for a more productive and happier stay in a foreign country.

Any knowledge gained prior to your departure to the country that you will be working in, full-time or part-time will be invaluable. Ask people who may have worked or visited there; while to some an archaic resource, don't forget the public library, you may be surprised

1

at what you can find there; *Google* it; delve through the *Lonely Planet* edition for the country that you be going to. I might add that a former colleague of mine made a significant contribution to *Lonely Planet* about Kazakhstan.

Keep an open mind and save the final judgment for yourself. Never, never, never go to a location with the pre-judgmental attitude that the foreign or "host" country will the same as your "home" country.

Complicating the difficulty of one's analysis of a foreign country is the various classifications of countries that one might find. For example, while a tad outdated model of the geopolitical world the grouping of countries classified as First World (that bloc of democratic-industrial countries within the sphere of American influence), Second World (that Eastern bloc of communist-socialist countries) and Third World (those countries not aligned with either of the aforementioned blocs) still rings in the mind of some post World War II analysts.

Roughly speaking, more current classification of the 195 countries in the world (plus or minus 2 or 3 depending on the time of the count) is centered on economic and human development. The *United Nations Development Program (UNDP) Report 2004* classifies 177 countries and areas as High Human Development, Medium Human Development and Low Human Development. The World Bank classification of 213 countries and regions is four tiered: High-Income economies; Upper-Middle Income economies; Lower-Middle Income economies; and, Low-Income economies. *The Financial Times* and the *London Stock Exchange (FTSE)* classify stock markets of 72 countries as Developed, Advanced Emerging, Secondary Emerging and Frontier.

Without getting into a detailed analysis of each it is safe to say that when one looks at a specific country it will fall within similar parameters, i.e. the United States falls within First World, High Human Development, High Income economy and Developed stock market while Kenya falls within Third World, Low Human Development, Low Income economy and Frontier stock market.

As a point of reference, throughout the rest of the discussions referring to comparisons of countries the three-tiered UNDP structure (See Appendix B) will be used.

Identifying where the country that you will be working is within these three categories will be helpful to you. Why? Because, and remember this because it is extremely important, you must not only adjust to the overseas work environment, but you must also adjust and adapt to the host country itself. Accepting the fact that it was you (in most cases anyway) who decided to work in a foreign country will help with the adjustment process.

Working overseas is not for everyone. The demands are greater and, in most cases so are the rewards. I have always believed that within any large organization, there is that special breed of people who thrive on the special challenges within the organization.

In the United States Army it's the Rangers, Airborne troops and Special Forces soldiers. In the construction industry it's the Drill & Blast guys and the Tunnel moles. In the United States government it's the overseas career diplomat or the USAID employee who believes that he can make a difference in making our world a better place to live in by helping administer U.S. Government humanitarian and development programs overseas. In the private business sector it's the bold, brash and cocky entrepreneurs, the risk takers and those people who work overseas.

This book is slanted towards an American working in an overseas environment. Why?—Because I'm an American and that's where my experience lies—over 35 years of it.

But remember that it may not be any easier for a Japanese to work outside of Japan or a Saudi outside of Saudi Arabia than it is for an American to work outside of the United States. What one leaves behind in all cases is his country, and in some instances his family and his friends. Sometimes the promise of big bucks is just not worth it.

This book will undoubtedly help you reach that decision as to whether or not to relocate overseas, if you have that choice. Additionally it will definitely help you to make those adjustments that you will need to make if you decide to work and/or live overseas. Some of the things discussed here will not only help you, the employee but they will help your family members as well.

There are various reasons one might choose to work outside of his own country whether for a long or a short period of time. Of the four that come to mind the first two; for career advancement and for money are driven by "I *have* to work overseas." The third and fourth; a belief that you can make a difference in the world though your organization's participation in the world arena and your desire to travel and explore different cultures are based less on greed or need than the first two. The last two are based on an attitude of "I *want* to work overseas."

Helen Keller said:

"Life is either a daring adventure or nothing."

Believe me; living and working overseas can be one daring and eye-opening adventure.

Sit back, relax and read on . . .

CHAPTER II

―――◈――

DEFINITIONS

FOR THE PURPOSE of this book, the following definitions apply:

Host Country: Any country that a company, or organization does business in other than where it has its' home office or headquarters.

Home country: The country that a company or organization has its' home office or headquarters in or which an employee is a citizen of.

Foreign National: A citizen of a host country.

Locally Employed Staff (LES): A foreign national hired employee working in their home country; also referred to as Foreign Service Nationals (FSNs) or Cooperating Country Nationals (CCNs).

Third Country National (TCN): An employee with a citizenship from a country other than that of the host country or the home country of the employing company; for example a Korean citizen working for an American company in Saudi Arabia.

Cultural Awareness: The awareness and recognition that people from different countries may have values, habits, customs, beliefs and behaviors that may be different from those found in other countries.

CHAPTER III

ABOUT THE AUTHOR, BY THE AUTHOR

FOR THOSE OF you who may not have read my first book, I am repeating the contents of Chapter II from it because you do have a valid question: *Who in God's name is David Anthony Korponai?*

"Before beginning this book, let me answer the one question that must be nagging some of you, "Who the hell is David Anthony Korponai?" This is a fair question that deserves an honest answer.

In a nutshell—After graduating from high school in Stratford, Connecticut I attended the University of Connecticut in Storrs. In addition to pursuing an education, I joined a fraternity (Alpha Sigma Phi), became involved in various campus activities and captained the UConn football team in my senior year.

My academic credentials upon graduation in June 1964 consisted of one year of general engineering courses (civil engineering was calling me my freshman year), one-half semester of general business courses; and two and one-half years of education courses which led to a Bachelor of Science degree in Physical Education.

During my junior year I was inducted into the ARCHONS, a service group of campus leaders. I also spent countless hours doing community service in the recreational program offered to residents in the town of Manchester, Connecticut. Through all of this, I did my utmost to make a positive contribution towards UConn's reputation as one of the top ten partying colleges and universities in America.

As an ROTC Distinguished Military Graduate, I accepted a regular Army appointment and was commissioned a 2nd Lieutenant in the United States Army. This was also in June 1964.

My fourteen year military career began when I was assigned as the Executive Officer for the Cooks School at Fort Dix, New Jersey—two days after graduating from UConn. This was followed, in rapid succession by my attendance of the Infantry Officer's Basic Course, Ranger School and Airborne School, all at Fort Benning, Georgia.

My overseas assignments, in order were Germany, Vietnam, Bolivia and again Vietnam.

My stateside assignments, in order, were Fort Dix, New Jersey; Fort Benning, Georgia; Fort Benjamin Harrison, Indiana, where, as a junior Captain I attended the Adjutants Generals Corp Advance Course; Fort Monmouth, New Jersey; and finally the Armed Forces Entrance and Examining Station in beautiful downtown Newark, New Jersey, where I was honorably discharged at the rank of captain in November 1978.

I spent almost six years in overseas assignments. I was awarded numerous letters of commendation and appreciation and two Bronze Star Medals for Meritorious Achievement, two Army Commendation Medals for Meritorious Achievement and two Joint Service Commendation Medals for Meritorious Achievement.

My most challenging and rewarding assignment was Chief of a Military Personnel Branch at Fort Monmouth, New Jersey, where, as a junior captain I filled this Major's position for more than two years. This branch was staffed by 105 men and women, both military and civilian.

My career in the private sector began in earnest in January 1979 when I returned to Bolivia with one wife, three young children, one dog and one cat—and, no job! Having sold our house in New Jersey and pooling resources, I gave myself six months to find gainful employment in the heart of South America.

I began this new adventure by accepting employment with the S.J. Groves & Sons Company. Groves & Sons was a large, Minneapolis based, American heavy construction company operating in Bolivia. They were building a forty-eight kilometer road from La Paz to Cotapata and a series of five bridges. I rose fairly quickly from a local hire with no fringe benefits, to the Administrative/Financial Manager, with full benefits for this 68 million U.S. dollar project.

Upon termination of the Groves & Sons project in April 1984, I was between jobs. I spent the next two years or so making ends meet by doing a variety of jobs which included consulting to several Bolivian companies, exchanging money and, on one occasion transporting dead, but plucked chickens from Cochabamba, to La Paz.

I also had a short stint of three months with the Narcotic's Assistance Unit of the American Embassy in La Paz, Bolivia. My title was the Coca Reduction Field Advisor and I spent most of my time in the largest coca growing area of Bolivia—the Chapare Valley in Cochabamba. Believe it or not, I recommended that this position be deleted! The reason—The program was so poorly designed that it was embarrassing to admit being a part of it as a U.S. Government employee; more about this later.

In August, 1986 I was hired by the R.A. Hanson Company (RaHCO) and served as their South American representative. This extremely innovative and well managed American company was based in Spokane, Washington. RaHCO was involved in mining and selling specialty equipment in the mining and heavy construction/earth moving sectors.

I represented RaHCO for almost two and one-half years. I traveled to Chile, Ecuador and Brazil evaluating business opportunities in the mining sector. When the owner, despite my protest decided to terminate his activities in South America rather than transfer the operation from La Paz, Bolivia, to Santiago, Chile where there was more potential and a more lucrative market I was again, between jobs. During this time I was asked to join, and accepted membership into the only English-speaking Masonic lodge in Bolivia, Anglo-Bolivian Lodge No. 7.

Having gone past my self-imposed time frame to find employment in Bolivia, I returned to the United States in late 1989 and found employment in Connecticut with a small, but highly successful industrial maintenance company, The Kaffen Company, Inc. I was employed as a working foreman. The company was mostly involved in concrete and tile floor repair and restoration and the painting of warehouses and storage tanks.

Believe me when I say that constructing scaffolding that reaches forty foot in height, operating a forty-foot extension boom or a jack hammer, scraping and grinding off old floor coatings on one's hands and knees, and smelling the pungent aroma of resins and acrylics is a far cry from the office environment. However, on the positive side it was a welcome relief from the doldrums of being unemployed.

While with the Kaffen Company I also learned something more about the management of human resources. I worked alongside the company's owner and CEO (a high school and college friend) and his three full-time employees. In addition, temporary hire employees, mostly wrenched from the inner-city work program were used.

The composition of our work group at any one time consisted of college graduates, high school graduates and drop outs and recovering or recovered alcoholics and substance abuse users. Interacting with and supervising this diverse work force at four o'clock in the morning was not only a test of one's managerial skills, but a test of one's character as well.

I also learned more about myself.

In January 1991, I applied for and was selected for the position of the General Services Officer for the United States Agency for International Development (USAID) mission in La Paz, Bolivia. My venture into the public sector began. I was fortunate enough to begin this career by working with, not for an executive officer who had vision, set high standards for himself and those who worked with him and was strongly committed to making the work environment a better place to work in. Improving quality of life in the workplace for employees was one of his major goals.

I managed a fifty-five person General Services Office. This customer focused position involved providing general logistical support to the Mission and its almost one hundred and fifty employees. The areas I managed included: customs; management of almost 4.5 million U.S. dollar's worth of non-expendable and expendable property and vehicles; real property management (leasing and maintenance of thirty-two houses and apartments); procurement of materials and services; and, vehicle support/motor pool activities.

Moving up, I then accepted the position of Deputy Executive Officer, in La Paz where I oversaw the General Services Office, the Personnel Office and the Missions' Communications and Records Office while acting as the alter ego to the Executive Officer during his absences. All of this was coupled with normal "deputy" type duties that included taking care of the daily business activities in the Executive Office, attending meetings that no one else wanted to attend and answering the telephone when the secretary was in the water closet.

Staying in the USAID family, I followed La Paz with over five years of service with USAID/Cairo Egypt as the Supervisory General Services Officer. This was, and still may be the largest USAID Mission in the world. When I arrived this Mission had over 100 apartments in its' housing portfolio and close to 400 American and Egyptian employees.

This was followed by almost eighteen months as the Executive Officer for USAID Almaty, Kazakhstan, a regional Mission supporting five countries; Kazakhstan, Uzbekistan, Tajikistan, Turkmenistan and Kyrgyzstan.

After a break in employment of about four months, I accepted the position as the Deputy Executive Officer for USAID Kiev, Ukraine. This large Mission was also regional and supported three countries; Ukraine, Moldova and

Belarus. I was again lucky enough to work with, not for a very creative and vibrant executive officer who had 'unlimited potential' written all over her. Her move from the Executive Officer ranks to upper management (Deputy Mission Director) positions proved me to be right on target.

After almost five years in Kiev I was selected for the Executive Officer position for the USAID Mission in Podgorica, Serbia/Montenegro. In addition to handling USAID business I also supervised the unit responsible for providing most of the administrative and logistical support to other agencies including the Department of State, Department of Commerce and Department of Defense.

When Montenegro gained her independence in May, 2006 I became involved in the unique and oftentimes overly bureaucratic exercise of transforming an American Consulate into a full-fledged American Embassy. And, the additional duty of a Department of State (DOS) Management Officer was thrust upon me. Being exposed to, and learning the DOS 'corporate culture' was challenging, exciting, rewarding and frustrating—all wrapped into one.

But to bring this to closure, I will note that damn near all of my assignments and positions that I held in the military and private and public sectors, in themselves and collectively turned out to be learning experiences, par excellence. There were many more positives than there were negatives.

I also discovered that there were a lot of people oriented, caring and professional executives and managers out there. Unfortunately, they did not vastly outnumber the ones who were narrow-minded, callous and self-centered and who put personal gains and career ahead of their office relationships and responsibilities (Keep note of this). Closing with a positive, I found that most people in either group had the talent, if not the motivation to become even more effective managers than they were."

That's verbatim from my first book. Since then I have had short term contracts with the USAID in Almaty, Kazakhstan, Kingston,

Jamaica and again in Almaty. As of this writing I am employed by the USAID/Jamaica on a two year contract.

Relax and read on, on your journey to becoming a more effective manager and adapting in a foreign country and overseas work environment.

CHAPTER IV

MORE EFFECTIVE MANAGEMENT AWARENESS ELEMENTS IN AN OVERSEAS ENVIRONMENT

BEFORE GETTING INTO the heart of this book, let me clarify and better define and reinforce two points:

At the risk of sounding *sexist*, as the English language has no neutral singular pronoun, I have used the words *he* and *she* in the text. It's easy. When you see a *he*, it could refer to a *he* or a *she*; when you see a *she* it could refer to a *she* or a *he*. And, a *him* could refer to a *him* or a *her*, and a *her* could refer to a *her* or a *him*. That's enough of Dr. Seuss' prosaic style. I hope that the use of these words is not only grammatically correct, but gender acceptable as well.

Once again, of the various country classifications defined in Chapter I, countries will be identified and mentioned or compared using the three-tiered UNDP structure of High, Medium and Low Human Development (Appendix B).

Adaptation

SPRECHEN SIE ENGLISH?
A More Effective Manager takes an interest in learning the host country language.

As mentioned in the introduction, this may not be applicable in all cases. As an English speaking native let me mention briefly what I have found in most foreign countries that I have worked in.

Most host country foreign national professionals will have a good knowledge of the English language. You can normally find a banker, attorney or doctor who speaks good English, especially in countries classified as High Human Development. Obviously the size of the city or town that you will be working in will have an influence on the number of people in this category.

The work environment is somewhat different. You will find that most managers and some supervisors and specialists will have some knowledge of the English language. Data management specialists, bank credit managers or loan officers and expediters are examples of people in this category. People in this category usually have a high school degree and at least two years of study in a university. Yet, it is not uncommon, especially in Medium and Low Human Development countries to have someone with a college degree working as a supply clerk or driver (more on this later).

Learn some street talk and every day phrases such as: "How much does this cost"?; "Take me to the airport" and, "Take me to the Ritz Hotel." Learn the numbers and some of the food dishes so you will not starve or eat bread for two weeks. And most of all learn how to say "Thank you", "You're Welcome" and "Please."

Be alert of words that may have a different meaning in a foreign country. In Arabic "zip/zib" means a male erection. In English "zip" means to put some excitement into or to add a little zest to your life. Being the gentleman that you are, it would still be somewhat awkward to offer to put a little "zip" to the office environment. Or how about saying to your secretary that; "I'd like to put a little "zip" into your life today". And, the female executive who asks the Egyptian businessman to use his "Zip-po" cigarette lighter will surely get a big smile!

Names are another area that can be testy. A Vietnamese surname is "Phuc" which is pronounced exactly like the nasty four-letter "f" word in English.

Abeer is a common Egyptian female name which is pronounced "A beer" rather than "Ah beer." I was in the office one holiday and I got a call from an American who was coming into the office with a female friend of his. He told me that the security guard needed my permission for him (the American) to bring Abeer into his office.

I told him that he does not need my permission to bring "A beer" into his office, all he has to do is put it in a bag and walk past the guard! This guy must have thought that I was upstairs sniffing glue. Anyway, he starts laughing and we get it straightened out.

Lastly, and maybe not slang but, noteworthy none the less as one more real experience. I am in Kiev trying to learn a bit more Russian. In America when someone sneezes it is common practice to say "God Bless You." In Russia, it is common practice to say "Bud' Zdorova" or "Be Healthy." To help me remember this I was taught a little jingle:

Bud' Zdorova
Rasti Kak Korova

This phrase when translated means: "Be Healthy, Grow like a cow."

So far so good—Until a rather buxom young lady working in the office happened to sneeze and I told her, with a big smile on my face and music ringing in my voice to, "Bud' Zdorova—Rasti Kak Korova" or "Be healthy—Grow like a cow"!

What people neglected to tell me was that this expression was used in the outlining villages and said to young kids, not adults; especially adults with rather large bosoms.

For native speaking English folks listening to someone speaking with a strong accent can sometimes put a smile on your face. Case in point—The American Cooperative School in La Paz used to host an informal get together for graduating seniors who planned to attend a college or university in the United States and students who were attending school in the US and back in La Paz for the holidays. Their parents were also invited to attend.

One conversation with three mothers went along the following lines.

Mother #1. My son is in Harvard and likes it very much.
Mother #2. My daughter is in Duke and studying to become a doctor.
Mother #3. My son is in Jale. He likes it and will be there three more jears.

What mother #3 said was: My son is in *Yale*. He likes it and will be there three more *years*.

Learning the local language (and the correct pronunciation of the names of your local staff) will show your foreign national staff that you are excited about working in their country and learning about it. It will enhance your image as a manager who is making an extra effort to communicate with them. Good luck—*Buena suerta*—*Haze said*—*Bon chance*—*Udacha*—*Viel gluck*

Be aware of the Importance of Learning the Host Country Language.

THE "UGLY AMERICAN" IMAGE:

A More Effective Manager is alert to the perceptions of others that surround both him, and the company or organization that he may work for.

While I use the term "Ugly American" as the example in this and in later discussions, as will be pointed as we move along labeling can cross into other nationalities as well.

How a foreign manager is perceived in the workplace is an important factor that will impact on her effectiveness. Believe it or not, bear in mind that in some cases how you are perceived in the community, outside of the workplace may also play a role in your capability to manage effectively.

Whether we agree with it or not persons tend to generalize about groups of people. If you are an American, you are well educated and have a lot of money. If you are a Latino, you are lazy and lack initiative. Unless you are a Latino in New York, then you can strip a car in ninety-seven seconds! If you are German, you are very precise and super organized. If you are British, you have a dry sense of humor and are very prim and proper. If you are Oriental, you are sly, sneaky and a hard worker. Can a Korean really swipe the spare tire off your jeep while you're driving 100 KPH down the highway?

The baggage that an American still carries in many places overseas, especially in the business community is one of being a ruthless, uncaring, and insensitive son-of-a-bitch who will stop at nothing to make as big a profit as possible and then leave. Americans do not have to, nor make long term commitments; thus, the "Ugly American" image. "Rape, pillage and plunder of the local work force" will be the cry of the local labor syndicates echoing throughout the land.

I may be exaggerating a tad here but, all of the above are truisms. Be prepared for it. One of the awareness elements that will be discussed in more detail later will be the role of the more effective manager in public relations.

Related to how you the individual is perceived remember to consider the company or organization image. Let me steal an example from my first book. I was the Coca Reduction Field Advisor for a U.S. Government (USG) agency in Bolivia. The goal was to reduce the number of hectares of coca that was being grown by offering growers monetary compensation based on the size of the land unit that they stopped growing the coca plant on. All of this sounded pretty simple and a great idea. It turned out to be not so simple and not such a good idea.

Keep in mind a base production area of one hectare and two or three crops per year. Picture this. The USG/GOB was offering anyone $200.00 for each hectare that they stopped growing the coca plant on. During the three months that I was assigned to the largest coca growing area in Bolivia, the commercial cash value, based on two crops per year and market prices of the dried coca leaf, for each hectare was about $3,000.00 per year. Picture this also. A fairly tall, good looking "Gringo" speaking suspect Spanish, with the help of a non-English speaking aide trying to sell this program to predominately non-Spanish speaking indigenous farmers who spoke Quechua.

These people may not have been well educated but they knew the difference between a deal based on a one-time receipt of $200.00 or continuing to gross $3,000.00 per year growing coca. When I got back to La Paz, I explained this to my boss and to the #2 person in the Agency in Washington who happened to be in La Paz at the time. Basically, I talked myself out of a job! For me to even try to implement a program with such a paltry offer was somewhat embarrassing, at least to me.

I am happy to say that I heard that a similar program was put in place based on a one-time payment of $2,000.00; crop substitution where growers are given replacement cash crop plants to grow like bananas, watermelons or artichokes; grower access to low interest capital to help improve their quality of life on the farm; and improved infrastructure to help foster and promote agro-industry projects. The USG now has, at least in my opinion, a better image in this geographic area.

Regardless of where your home office is, or what your nationality is you are still a "foreigner" to host country nationals. It is imperative that you, the more effective manager develop a reputation of impeccable character based on fairness, honesty, and integrity. Keep chipping away at the stereo-typed image that you may have by educating the indigenous people in your work force.

Wages are a sensitive issue especially in the private sector. The exploitation of the local workforce once again surfaces. How do you combat this? You pay a *fair* wage for services rendered. Check with your local embassy, if one exists in country or some of the local organizations like the Chamber of Commerce.

When I was working in Cairo the USAID had a local contractor running its warehousing operation. However, they were experiencing a high turnover of warehouse staff. This was directly attributable to the wages that the company was paying. Needless to say this worker turnover had a negative impact on the General Services operations that I was supervising. Each new employee had to get a security certification. Getting this certification took time and oftentimes the labor force was short staffed.

The solution was to come up with a salary somewhere between what a local would make if he were employed by an Egyptian company and what a person employed in a similar position by the USAID would make. While cutting a bit into his profit margin the Contractor agreed and it was a win-win situation as the Contractor saved some money by having to pay less overtime and fewer employee termination benefits.

Speaking of wages, and to stray a tad; two comments about wages. I recently read an article about Cuba. Unemployment is almost zero. One reason for this is that so many people are "employed" by the state. The article went on to describe, and picture this: four guys digging a ditch; one digging the ditch, one standing and leaning on his shovel waiting his turn to dig the ditch; one sleeping in a wheel barrel in the shade; and one supervising. The moral of the story—The State pretends to pay us, and we pretend to work!

Did you hear the old Russian joke about State pensioners? A man walks up to the window to get his paltry pension and is told that there are no funds and to come back tomorrow. The man shows up the next day and walks up to the same window. The guy behind the window looks up at him and says "What are you doing here today, I told you to come back tomorrow."

Labor issues have no boundaries and from some of the horror stories coming out of China it seems like Chinese laborers in China and those in Medium and Low Human Development (MHD/LHD) countries are where American laborers were 50 or 100 years ago—low wages and sweat-shop like conditions especially for unskilled workers. You hear of cheap labor and exploitation of workers in these countries many times over. If the AFL/CIO were to take a real interest in influencing the "working class" (like wealthy people don't work?) they should be spending more time, energy and money in these countries. But, it is probably not too easy to get into countries like China, North Korea or Cuba or a host of other MHD and LHD countries.

At the risk of sounding like an "I told you so" guy I have recently observed the influence that China is exerting in many sectors of business and industry in other countries. Many Chinese families have integrated and settled in a host of High, Medium and Low Development Countries and through hard work have done very well for themselves. You can probably find a Chinese restaurant, dry cleaners or sundry shop in darn near ever country in the world. Nonetheless, it seems to me that the new, high powered, mega-rich and influential Chinese players, especially those in the private sector are going down a path that, if it hasn't done so already will eventually lead to the "Ugly Chinese" image.

Be Aware of the "Ugly American" Image and How You Are Perceived by Others.

A GUEST IN SOMEONE ELSE'S COUNTRY:

A More Effective Manager understands that no matter how much money his company or organization is investing into a host country or how much they are contributing to its' development, he is still a "guest" in that country.

This ties in with several awareness elements addressing the Ugly America image and cultural sensitivity.

All host country residents may not extend their hospitality towards you, but the vast majority of them will; especially those in the office or shop that you supervise. Reciprocity to that hospitality by respecting host country laws and customs and traditions, for example is a must. We'll get into a more detailed look at these later on.

Suffice to say now that if you project the image of a pompous, up and coming, high flying executive or a blue-blooded bureaucrat who thinks that their poop smells like roses you will have a real problem on your hands; a maelstrom of your own making I might add.

Remember the old saying, "I may be slow but I ain't stupid." While some of your "hosts" may be less educated than you are they will undoubtedly have a lot more street smarts than you can imagine. You are on someone else's turf and playing in someone else's backyard.

Will acceptance of this help you become a more effective manager and help you adapt in a foreign country? You bet your sweet bippy it will. You will get more respect from not only the people in your place of work, but from those outside of it as well. Keep fixated in this area.

Be Aware That You Are a Guest in Someone Else's Country.

SOCIAL INTEGRATION:
A More Effective Manager adapts to and integrates himself into social, as well as business activities in the host country.

There are many reasons for this. One is to help you and your family to get a better feeling for the local customs and traditions. Another is, it will help you get into a comfort zone; a zone that will allow you and your family members to feel more free to move around within the city or countryside.

In Bolivia for instance it is customary to *challa* or to bless certain things like new vehicles or newly acquired property or events such as the start of a construction project, the completion of a roof, etcetera. Simple enough, right?

In the case of a vehicle *challa*, one decorates the vehicle with paper streamers and the manager and principle driver and friends spill some cane alcohol and beer on various parts of the vehicle, normally the tires. Have a barbeque or sandwiches and some refreshments of beer or drinks and you have the complete picture. *Challa* your vehicle and your neighbors will love you.

If you are drinking beer, after you pop the top spill a little on the ground first, to bless the *pacha mama* or mother earth and the workers will love you even more! Social integration can help you understand a country's culture and customs—to help you fit in with your new neighbors.

Sports clubs or social clubs are good places to help you on your way to social integration. Don't forget the Chamber of Commerce or other business associations. Fraternal organizations like the Order of Freemasons provide excellent avenues for you to not only socialize, but to vent some of your frustrations as well.

If you are married with children, integrating into the local community can also have a profound impact on the life of your family, especially the children. Kids, especially between the ages of three and six have a tendency to pick up a new language faster than their parents. At any age, learning a second of third language will be a big plus in later life.

If you have children who may go to your home country sponsored school similar to an American sponsored school, a German School or a French School participate in their activities. These schools normally have a nice mixture of host country, home country and third country national children. Maybe a stint on the school board is in order. And don't forget to get your spouse involved.

When I returned to Bolivia in 1978 our twins were eight years old and our oldest son was ten. They were fluent in the Spanish language by the time that they were teenagers. Likewise, the Bolivian friends that they made in school helped me expand my social awareness. I also made several business contacts that I later put to good use.

Social integration will help you on the job by showing your local employees that you take an interest in not only them, but in their compatriots as well. And, as already mentioned it will also help in your local networking and to develop contacts that may facilitate your managing.

Be Aware of Getting Socially Involved With the Local Populace.

SERVICES—LIGHTS OUT:

A More Effective Manger identifies areas where services may be marginal at best.

This includes either private or state provided utility services such as electricity, water, telephone, gas and sewerage. Repair and maintenance of vehicles, appliances and electronics and residential maintenance and repair work are other areas included here that may offer only limited services.

The first group is important in both the work and home environment. The disruptions caused in the work place by power shortages, blackouts, or brownouts goes without saying. If you are in manufacturing, will a back-up generator solve this problem?

I was told that not too long ago in Cairo telephone service was so poor that an unskilled person was hired to do nothing but dial the telephone to get a line—within the city limits! It was faster to deliver a message across town by messenger than it was to place a call across town. Cairo at that time had a population of nearly 12 million inhabitants. Get the feeling of isolation?

It was not uncommon for power outages to last for two or three days in La Paz, Bolivia in the early 1980s. One solution—Take a day off and have a barbeque with friends so that the meat would not spoil. It was impossible to get those IBM electric typewriters in the office fired up without juice. Has it gotten better since then—I'm disappointed to report, not very much.

Area grid electrical outages were very common in Kiev, Ukraine; at least in the grid where my apartment was. The elevator in the apartment building that I lived in had a cabin a tad larger than a telephone booth. It was wire mesh enclosed all four sides and had a capacity to hold four rather slim people. While there are not very many slim Ukrainians four managed to snuggle up together even with their wet winter coats on and the ladies carrying their *sumkas* (handbags) and packages. A telephone call to the local Otis dealer normally meant that someone would come with the master key in an hour or so.

I got stuck in the cabin my fair share of the time when the electricity went out but, as luck would have it most often it was when I was carrying a six pack of *Baltica* the Russian *pivo* (beer). I usually popped one for myself and offered to share my stock with my fellow riders. The effort that they made to make me feel more comfortable by trying to speak English while I was trying to speak Russian actually made me feel good and, the time passed more quickly.

Talking about electricity, make sure you find out about local voltage and cycles. There are many countries that only have 220 Volt, 50 cycle service. Most small and kitchen appliances in the United States are 110 Volt, 60 cycles. The 50 cycles output will cause a slowdown in electric clocks and small appliances such as hairdryers and blenders. Timers in ovens may also be affected.

I knew a new young bride married to an Army officer assigned to a unit in Germany. This was their first time overseas and Thanksgiving Day arrived. The thought of a succulent, moist turkey dinner was interrupted by the sight of smoke billowing out of the oven and the smell of burning skin. While the bird had a rich carbon color on the outside and was a bit dry on the inside a good time was had by all, especially after the second or third bottle of Liebfraumilch wine and a few peppermint schnapps.

Knowledge of areas in a host country where services might be marginal or even lacking will help you, the more effective manger better exercise some control of these wherever you are working. This knowledge, when passed on to family members will help immeasurably in their adaptation to a new country and lifestyle.

Be Aware of the Import of Identifying Marginally Serviced Areas.

MISSING AMENITIES:

A More Effective Manager accepts the fact that amenities, those things that add to your material comfort or convenience normally found in High Human Development countries will not be found in some other countries in the world.

Some of you will pick-up on this theme in other discussion topics but this brief adds emphasis to the bottom line: You may have to do without some of the things that you are accustomed to having.

Those of you in the military or U.S. Government sectors that have Post Exchange privileges or commissary privileges may not require much of an adjustment. You can always get frozen vegetables and Baskin and Robbins ice cream and pizza trays and lip gloss and fabric softener. And most countries have reciprocal agreements between them that allows for diplomats to bring in items duty free from their home country.

But let's take a quick look at the missing amenities in both the work and living environment. Not being able to buy an air conditioning unit in Cairo is a bitch as is not being able to find any screens for your office or residence windows in Manila in July.

The primary heating system was central hot water in Almaty, Kazakhstan several years ago. Older flats and offices had hot water radiators. However, in many instances the radiators did not have a shut-off control valve that worked. Thermostats were non-existent. The solution in the winter time when it became too hot in the room was to—you guessed it—open up a window! I am happy to report that nowadays the newer places have HVAC units. Split pack AC/heating units are also common for individual rooms and in most cases readily available on the local market.

Overcoming these obstacles will help you to become a more effective manager. How? Accepting things like these, and putting up with them if you can't change them will give you a better image with the foreign nationals in the work environment. You will not be viewed as a pompous, pampered and privileged foreigner. If you can find an air conditioning unit or window screens or a water cooler or a flushing mechanism for the old toilet in the malodorous office water closet you will be viewed upon as a manager who *cares* about the work force and the work environment. The more you can do to improve the work environment, or services within the work environment the more you will be perceived as a more effective manager.

Look for ways to expand services to your fellow employees. Think outside of the box. Providing a shuttle service to American employees utilizing passenger vans is common practice in a lot of embassies and USAID Missions. This is normally at a nominal cost to the employee. Routes may be varied for security reasons but door to door service is still the rule. Locally Employed Staff (LES) are sometimes provided with a stipend to help defray public transportation costs.

The American embassy in Jamaica leases a parking lot fairly close to the embassy compound to accommodate LES who drive to work. A shuttle zips back and forth for this 10 minute round trip ride at pre-determined, scheduled times.

Once again, welcome to the real world of working in an overseas environment.

Be Aware of Missing Amenities and How Living Without Them May Affect Your Mood and Your Ability to Adjust in a Foreign Country.

DOMESTIC HELP:

A More Effective Manager welcomes the employment of domestic help that is available in the host country.

Same question, right? "Why in the world should a more effective manager be concerned about domestic help"? The common sense answer is peace of mind. Again, this may not be applicable to those of you going to a High Human Development country like Austria or Canada

You may be surprised to find that whether you are single, or married your ability to manage or reduce the petty frustrations that might arise outside of the work environment will have a very positive effect on your performance on the job.

If you are coming from a High Human Development country to a Medium or Low Human Development country, the adjustment will be even more profound. No automatic dishwashers in Cairo. "When was the last time that you had dishpan hands"?

You can't drink the tap water in Bangladesh. "When was the last time you boiled and filtered water before drinking it"?

They used to fertilize some fields in Germany from "Honey wagons". When was the last time you soaked lettuce in iodine before eating it? Incidentally, honey wagons collect the "natural fertilizer" that animals and humans excrete every so often; unless more frequently if you have Montezuma's Revenge from drinking the tap water that you neglected to boil and filter!

If you are in a position to do so, treat yourself a little. Look into hiring domestic help. How about a cook who can not only cook, but who can clean the smelly fish you catch and make the best sushi that you ever tasted and do your grocery shopping to boot? A gardener may help to trim the roses and spread the fertilizer from the honey wagon. Get the name of a good handyman to fix those leaky faucets, do some minor electrical work and maybe even do some painting.

Domestic help can also help you or your spouse in doing errands such as paying bills or delivering invitations. They know the local markets, especially the outdoor food markets. Fresh vegetables, fruits and meats for those succulent meals that are ready and waiting for you when you get home.

Speaking of fresh, I was in the local market in La Paz one afternoon when someone who did not speak a word of Spanish asked me if the eggs were fresh. I said, "For sure, they still have the chicken sh!t on them."

Most domestic help is garnered through word of mouth and personal recommendations. Unless you personally know the person recommending the domestic help be sure to do a reference check on whomever it is you intend to hire. Another source of referrals may be found at your local embassy.

For all you gourmet chefs who hire a local cook, as an added bonus think of all the new local recipes that you can add to your international cook book.

Be Aware of Discovering and Employing Domestic Help in the Host Country.

HEALTH CARE:

A More Effective Manager is knowledgeable of the health care services and facilities available in a host country.

Remember the Greek philosophy of sound mind and sound body.

Let's start with one of the wisdoms credited to the great American statesman Benjamin Franklin:

> *"In wine there is wisdom,*
> *In beer there is freedom*
> *In water there is bacteria."*

Believe it or not, there are still some countries out there where tap water is safe to drink. None-the-less, according to Ben if you don't want to drink the water that leaves you with two choices; drink wine or drink beer. But, buying and drinking imported bottled water at 3 or 4 times the price of a bottle of beer might be a third choice. Speaking of bottled water, I recently read that 25% of all bottled water was in fact, regular tap water. Or, when was the last time that you boiled water to make it potable?

Could a bad case of Montezuma's revenge lead to more serious problems and an urgent need to become familiar with host country facilities? Maybe, so be prepared. Know where the nearest pharmacy is (You better learn to read this one in the host country language).

Let's ratchet this up a notch or two and move on to facilities and systems in country.

You will find that in Low Human Development countries that while many physicians have studied or have had some training in the United States or Europe, and are very competent and professional people, the follow-up care by nurses and interns, such as post-operative care is questionable. Also uncertain is the cleanliness of facilities and equipment.

Case in point—I knew someone who had a minor operation performed in La Paz, Bolivia that required anesthesia. He was being moved from the operating room to the recovery room after it was over. No gurney. According to his wife, he was carried in a blanket, one intern on each of the corners, with his arms and legs dangling over the sides and dragging along the floor. Someone missed the vein with the intravenous needle and his arm swelled up to the size of his thigh before it as noticed.

In the end, he was up and around in a few days. The surgeon was superb and the surgery went off with nary a hitch. For a hundred and forty-nine bucks, what can you expect, right?

Dental care is a specialty that can be outrageously expensive even in Low Development countries. This is especially true for fees charged to foreigners. The costs of procedures at the dental clinic used by most ex-patriots or recommended by an embassy may be damn near equal to those found in the United States. This is true from fillings to root canals to crown works. There are rare exceptions to this for sure.

When I was in Kiev I lived across the street from a dental clinic that was used by local students and retired folks. Fillings were seven bucks a pop. I think that they may have used watered down road patch, but mine are still in place.

Envision this: Dental chairs were lined up five abreast. After poking around the dentist pulled out the drill and revved it up. I asked her if she was going to give me a shot of Novocain. She asked me if it hurt and when I told her *nyet* she said: "No hurt, no Novocain." When she told me to spit, the bowl looked like a spittoon, complete with spit,

Solving Management's Puzzle • David Korponai

yellow hawkers, blood and bloody gauze and cotton wads and God only knows what else.

Three of her friends came in and started talking and eating liverwurst and onion sandwiches while she was still working on me. They were talking up a storm and having a good time. When she finished and took off her mask and smiled at me it looked like she had not been to a dentist in a long long time. How could I tell? The few jagged *zubie* (teeth) and brown stains on those that that were still in her mouth were a dead giveaway. The positive side—seven bucks and she was right—I did not need the Novocain.

And don't forget to ask about the availability of prescription drugs and medication. Can you find a substitute drug or medicine at the local pharmacy? Do you need a prescription to purchase locally? In some countries drugs available only by prescription may be sold over the counter in others.

Access to a medical facility may also be an issue so check this out soon after arriving. I was told that to access a hospital or clinic in Cairo, to include the emergency room that you had to pre-pay, in cash certain fees. For those of you who are considering working in Egypt and your mind-set is to rely primarily on credit cards, you may have to change it.

How about checking your company's health insurance plan? Does the plan provide for emergency medical evacuation and if so, is it all the way back to your home country, or only to the nearest *adequate* facility. Does it include dental coverage?

Try to learn and understand about the health care system for the local employees as well. Especially if most of them use the public sector, government run facilities. It will undoubtedly take longer to diagnose and treat illnesses if someone is in the state system. It is not unusual for an employee to wait hours for an initial check-up and then to be passed around to other places to get an x-ray or to get lab work done. How will this affect the work flow in your section?

Maternity leave policy, established by the host government may also bring surprises and have regulated pre and post-natal care policies that are mandated by a Local Leave and Compensation Plan (More on this later).

An awareness of health care services in the host country will not only give you a sense of serenity, but also alert you to possible management issues in the workplace. This alone will contribute to your understanding of the work environment and becoming a more effect manager.

Be Aware of the Availability and the Limitations of Local Health Care Services and Facilities.

HOUSING CONDITIONS/STANDARDS:

A More Effective Manager keeps an open-mind when searching for housing.

Right—How is your awareness of local housing conditions and standards going to help you manage more effectively? Excellent question and since the subject is so broad I touched on the answer to this in other discussion topics but it deserves separate recognition at this time.

The one answer that I can think of is that your awareness and acceptance of local housing conditions and standards will give you more tranquility when you get to work. Happy at home, happy in the work environment will be the end result.

I said *acceptance* of local housing conditions and standards. Building codes vary dramatically from country to country, especially in the areas of plumbing and electrical works.

If you have the time, go over your living accommodations (apartment, house or whatever) with someone knowledgeable in the trades areas related to building construction or maintenance. If you do not have the time, make the time!

Upgrade as much as possible those areas that will make you as comfortable as possible when you return from work. If you are married get your spouse involved; especially with color schemes of walls and ceilings, kitchen layout, condition of floors, etcetera. Remember that most times your spouse, or companion will spend more time at home than you will. Use your negotiating skills to get as much work done and paid for by the owner. You will be surprised how accommodating some will be. Consider cost-sharing; you pay for the materials and the owner pays for labor or vice versa.

And don't forget to address any security needs at this time. Decorative grill work on the windows, for example. How about consideration of apartment living only above the second floor? Installation of Mylar on the inside of windows facing the street may be called for in some countries deemed high on the list of terrorist activities. Again—peace of mind.

Also if your company employees an number of "ex-pats" from your country, equality in housing may become an issue that can effect ex-pat morale and job performance. No kidding! Are you forced to live in company furnished leased housing or can you go out and find your own place? Will you have to live in a company compound?

When I was working for the S.J. Groves Company in Bolivia, married workers were allowed to, and encouraged to live in a house or an apartment. They were given a rent stipend based on the number of family members living with them. They were given this money and were on their own to find and negotiate a lease. Most employees found housing within the La Paz area that was about a one-hour drive from the work site.

Bachelors on the other hand were provided individual rooms in a barracks type building at the camp site. Several multi-bedroom apartments were leased by the company in the downtown area of La Paz where they could spend a rare day off.

As mentioned above, remember that in most Low Human Development countries building codes are almost nonexistent. Units built over seismic zones will, in all probability fall like a house of cards.

What's more, for those of you going to any number of the ex-Soviet union countries apartment complexes are normally only five stories high and with no elevators. You might want to think twice about the fifth floor apartment and consider things like what it will be like lugging groceries up five flights of very dimly lit stairs that are in dire need of repair.

Speaking of which, there were some old apartment buildings in Cairo with the same characteristics; i.e. five-stories high and no elevator. I attended a party one night on the third floor and I noticed the host, and friend of mine on the balcony with a basket tied to a rope. He'd lower the basket; yell his order to the store owner below who would then fill the basket with goodies which my friend would hoist back up to the balcony. It worked fine for both the buyer and the seller.

Believe me, an awareness of host country housing conditions and standards, and acceptance of these will add to your managerial effectiveness in the work environment. And once again it will play a significant role in spousal or partner and family adjustment.

Be Aware of Local Housing Conditions and Construction Standards.

YOUR SPOUSE OR PARTNER:

A More Effective Manager is compassionate towards the adjustment that their spouse or partner may have to make in the host country and the impact that it will have on his attitude and ability to focus in the work environment.

This is not a one gender area of consideration. I have seen in overseas environments where the house-*husband* had just as difficult a time adjusting as the house-*wife*. Not to be aware of this element will contribute to one's unhappiness and possible marital problems.

Most foreign countries, especially Medium and Low Human Development countries do not have as many leisure time activities as found in High Human Development countries. In the area of sports, for example there were only two decent bowling alleys in Cairo, Egypt. Cairo had a population of 14 million people. There is only one golf course in La Paz, Bolivia. What could happen? A person could become bored. You could turn into a couch potato. Worst yet, boredom could lead to discontentment or depression, which could lead to the bitch, bitch, bitch syndrome or to excessive drinking or carousing around the neighborhood. Worst yet, a strained relationship develops which could lead to marital problems. Don't laugh. This is not an unreal scenario. The above can happen to either the employee or the spouse or partner.

Let's focus on you, the wage earner for a brief moment. I know several employees who got so wound up and wrapped up in their work and became oblivious to this awareness element that their marriages failed. They became an enigma to their spouse and other family members. Hang in there. Try not to become "career dependent." Do not bring the office to the home, or the home to the office. However, bring your peace of mind to the office knowing that whomever you live with also has their peace of mind at home.

Let's flash back to the spouse/partner. How about one that is used to working? Employment opportunities may be scarce, especially if they have a profession. This needs to be considered even before your acceptance of an overseas position. Your contract with your employer does not obligate him to employ your spouse/partner, or any other family members for that matter. This may sound insensitive, but the employee, not the spouse has the contract with the company.

However, some organizations may, similar to the U.S. Government hire tandem couples. Both are employed by the USG. Every effort is made to post them to the same location; i.e. Berlin, Almaty or wherever.

The USG also has a program that favors hiring qualified spouses for certain positions. The Community Liaison Officer is a good example of this. These folks normally publish a newsletter with information about the host country and local events. Other functions include organizing trips, many of which are family oriented, setting up a library and screening local domestic help.

You also have the situation where family members may not be allowed to accompany the employee to the overseas destination. This is especially true for people working in high, potentially explosive and unpredictable areas such as Pakistan or Afghanistan. And after your evaluation of your options you may decide not to take them even if you could. You are then thousands of miles away from one another.

Many of you may have picked up the family theme, which includes all dependents. Of prime consideration is schooling for school aged children. Many countries do not have adequate secondary schools and boarding school, or home-schooling may be the only way to go. One must give careful thought and consideration to spouse and family needs before deciding on accepting employment overseas. Is the risk of detaching one's self from the family really worth it? You are the only one who can answer that question.

Be Aware of the Influence That Spousal/Partner Adjustment Can Have on Your Adapting in Country and the Attitude That You Bring Into the Workplace.

TERRORISM/CRIME:

A More Effective Manager never loses sight of the possibility that acts of terrorism or crime can occur anywhere in the world.

Don't panic! For those of you accepting employment in a country with a history of terrorist activities you must prepare yourself and your family both mentally and physically for a move there. But remember, there is not a single country in the world that is exempt from possible acts of terrorism. Witness the incident at the World Trade Center in New

York City on 26 February, 1993 in which a truck bomb was detonated below the North Tower, the bombing at the Alfred P. Murrah Federal Building in downtown Oklahoma City on 19 April, 1995 in which a truck filled with explosives was detonated in front of the building and the tragedy that struck the World Trade Center again in New York City on 11 September, 2001 in which two hi-jacked commercial airlines were flown into the twin towers. There have been acts of terrorism in virtually every country in the world; be they High, Medium or Low Human Development countries.

While acts of terrorism are more correctly defined as those acts of terror aimed at a specific government or group, you should also bear in mind that while some countries may appear to be low risk as far as terrorist activities are concerned, they may have a high rate of violent crime such as murder or armed robbery. The risk of being killed or wounded by a stray bullet in these situations may be higher than the risk of a terrorist incident.

What heightens the anxiety level for foreigners living in countries where a "terrorist" act might occur is the fact that the employee's company or people of his nationality may, in fact become a targeted group for the terrorists. Thus the "Yankee Go Home", anti-Christian campaign in some Muslim countries or anti-Muslim campaign in some Christian countries become focal points. You, the more effective manager must look for ways to keep the workplace as safe an environment as you possibly can.

Your awareness in this area will help you to have more composure in the work environment. This stems from knowing that you have prepared yourself and your family members to be aware of and primed for terrorist type activities and criminal acts should they occur.

Being alert in crowds, putting an extra lock on the door or windows, varying your route to work and installing a security alarm system are just a few of the security precautions that one should consider.

Does your company have an evacuation plan? Does your compensation include hazardous duty pay? Does your firm care about your physical security? A more effective manager will focus on, assess, and evaluate the *threat level* (low-medium-high) in the country that he is contemplating working in. If an individual feels that he and his family will be able to cope with this level the chances of success in the overseas work environment will surely be greatly enhanced.

Related to this bigger picture is becoming familiar with the places, zones and areas to stay away from. Most large cities, regardless of the country have areas like this. Stay away from the tourist traps and mind the way that you dress. Avoid standing out like that sore thumb.

I remember several years ago, German tourists were targets in the Miami, Florida area. The tactic that was used most centered on carjacking and road crime.

For you hot-shot, single guys' watch out for the night club scams that normally center around buying watered down drinks either for yourself and/or for some long legged chick who happens to speak your language. Spiked drinks that make you feel woozy and light-headed just before closing time may lead you right to an expensive taxi ride or worst yet, a ride to the countryside where you may be relieved of your wallet and your clothes.

In all honesty, if you feel that this risk is too great, stay at home, read my first book and practice your more effective management skills in an environment that you feel more secure and comfortable in.

Be Aware of the Possibility of Coming Face-to-Face With Terrorist Activity or Criminal Acts at Any Time.

STRESS MANAGEMENT
A More Effective Manager learns how to cope with the additional stress that is placed on her when working in an overseas environment.

Having discussed the above areas that one must be aware of in the overseas work environment let me bring this section to closure by briefly mentioning the stress factor.

Notwithstanding stress that you may feel while working in your home country at your "normal" place or work, I strongly believe that the overseas environment places additional strain on an employee. There is just more tension and anxiety in this arena.

There are literally hundreds of resources from books to DVDs to newspaper articles to seminars that one can read, listen to or purchase that can help him deal with stress. Most begin by mentioning the need to identify the source of your stress. I recently read one unidentified article that listed and discussed six stress management strategies:

1.   *Avoid unnecessary stress.*
2.   *Alter the Situation.*
3.   *Adapt to the stress.*
4.   *Accept the things that you can't change.*
5.   *Make time for fun and relaxation.*
6.   *Adopt a healthy life style.*

How do you deal with this additional stress so far away from your country and home office and possibly from your family and friends? Let me quote from an Email I recently received on the internet from a friend of mine:

"A lecturer, when explaining stress management to an audience, raised a glass of water and asked, 'How heavy is this glass of water?' Answers called out ranged from 8 oz. to 20 oz.

The lecturer replied, 'the absolute weight doesn't matter. It depends on how long you try to hold it.

'If I hold it for a minute, that's not a problem. If I hold it for an hour, I'll have an ache in my right arm.

If I hold it for a day, you'll have to call an ambulance.

'In each case it's the same weight, but the longer I hold it, the heavier it becomes.

He continued, 'And that's the way it is with stress management. If we carry our burdens all the time, sooner later, as the burden becomes increasingly heavy, we won't be able to carry it.

'As with the glass of water you have to put it down for a while and rest before holding it again. When we're refreshed, we can carry on with the burden.

'So before you return home tonight, put the burden of work/life down. Don't carry it home. You can pick it up tomorrow.

'Whatever burdens you're carrying now, let them down for a moment if you can. Relax; pick them up later after you've rested.

Life is short. Enjoy'!

Avoiding stress may be one of those, "easier said than done" kind of things. However, just being aware of the fact that additional stress may be forthcoming in an overseas work environment will help ease your tension and anxiety and offer relief that will pay huge dividends for you in both the short and the long runs.

Relaxation is certainly a key ingredient here. Getting involved in community, school or church activities are ways to reduce the stress. Indulging in a hobby or physical activity are both ways to lessen the tightness and apprehension that might be gnawing away at your physical and mental health. Relaxing through meditation or yoga are also ways that come to mind. Incorporate these into you daily regime; stay calm, cool and collected and you are well on your way on a positive path to stress management.

Be Aware of the Need to Apply Stress Management Techniques in Your Daily Routine.

Host Country Environment

RELIGIOUS CUSTOMS:

A More Effective Manager is tolerant of, and shows respect to religious customs in a host country.

There is really not much to say here. An awareness of these may even help you in the work place by getting you to focus on work flow during religious holiday periods. A striking example of this is Ramadan a major religious holiday in the Muslim faith. It is characterized by fasting from sunrise to sunset for normally twenty-eight consecutive days. The daily period of fasting starts at the breaking of dawn and ends at the setting of the sun. Muslims totally abstain from food, drink, smoking and sex during the dawn and daylight hours. The usual practice is to have a pre-fast meal (*suhoor*) before dawn and a post-fast meal (*iftar*) after sunset.

It is not uncommon for real individual productivity in the workplace to decline by 35-50% during this period. Employees may become lethargic, fall asleep at their desk, or become down-right irritable.

I was working in Cairo and it was Ramadan. The American supervisor, who was a section leader supervising four Foreign Service National staff and whom I was supervising came into my office one day with a handful of unsigned leave slips. I asked who they were for and he told me that they were for the local employees he caught sleeping at their desks. This guy timed this down-time and wanted to charge these people annual leave. Maybe he was right. However, to me this was not a question of right or wrong but what one must accept as a fact of life in the "real world" that we manage in.

Was it fair to the ones who managed to stay awake all day? Good question. I asked a dozen or so of the other local staff for their opinion and it was unanimous—"It's OK Mr. David, they work very hard when they are not sleeping."

Muslins pray five times each day. The times vary slightly depending on the time of sunrise. For planning purposes they are normally at: sunrise; noon; once in the afternoon; sunset; and, once again in the evening. Some companies may set aside prayer rooms for their Muslin employees.

This prayer time may be seen by some as similar to some Christians who pray four times each day, once before each meal and once before they go to bed.

In Saudi Arabia, I have been told that virtually everything stops during prayer times. This includes meetings and interviews and work. Friday is the holy day.

The work week in a Muslin country is from Sunday through Thursday. In Egypt, for most Egyptian companies and the government of Egypt and the American Embassy and other USG agencies, this Sunday through Thursday work schedule was followed.

Religious holidays in Latin America may be celebrated a bit differently between countries. But one, Carnival, the pre-lent time for merrymaking and festivals in the Roman Catholic faith is world famous in most large cities to include Rio de Janeiro, Brazil and Oruro, Bolivia. And for those of you who may be assigned to the United States check out New Orleans at this time of the year.

I recently read that Druidry, the ancient Celtic pagan faith is now a recognized religion in England. To better understand this one must know the fact that it is widely practiced in England and note that:

According to a passage in a Wikipedia essay on Druidry (since deleted):

> *"Modern Druidism (a.k.a. Modern Druidry) is a continuation of the 18th-century revival and is thus thought to have some, though not many, connections to the Ancient Religion. Modern Druidism has two strands, the cultural and the religious. Cultural Druids hold a competition of poetry, literature and music known as the Eisteddfod amongst the Celtic peoples (Welsh, Irish, Cornish, Breton, etc.). Modern religious Druidry is a form of Neopaganism built largely around writings produced in the 18th century and later, plus the relatively sparse Roman and early medieval sources."*

Cahan Tiarnan, writing about religious Druidry, said:

> *"Contrary to wrong beliefs, Druids have always been and still are religious, not only believing in, but also knowing reincarnation is real. Furthermore, Druids know there are many Gods and Goddesses. One cannot be a 'Christian, Wiccan, Moslem or anything else' and a Druid. They will contradict each other."*

Druid rituals involve "commonality of practice" across the faith including solar and fire festivals, ceremonies at various phases of the moon, seasonal festivals and rites of passage in life. How any Druid religious holidays will fit into recognition of official religious holidays in England still remains to be seen.

Those of you who are Druids take note. Maybe pitching for an assignment to England is in order.

Be Aware of, and Respectful of Host Country Religious Customs.

CLASS STRUCTURE:

A More Effective Manager recognizes that in some Medium and in Most Low Human Development countries there basically exists a two tiered class structure.

It's not that difficult to see either: the elite or upper class and the lower class. These are sometimes still brought up in conversations and referred to as the "Haves" and the "Have Not's."

In High Human Development countries there exists a multi-tiered class structure; the three pronounced being the elite or upper class, the middle class and the lower class. Within this multi-tiered structure you may have further breakdowns identified by the adjectives upper, middle or lower as in: upper upper class; middle upper class; lower upper class; upper middle class; middle middle class; lower middle class; upper lower class; middle lower class or whatever.

Let's focus the rest of this discussion on the first, two-tiered group. Visualize a pyramid—a compressed pyramid. There are very few people in the point or little nipple at the top. The majority of people are in the broad, bloated base of the pyramid—the masses.

Why should you, the more effective manager be aware of this? I can think of at least two good reasons. One is that host country national employees will normally view you, and mostly all foreigners as being in the elite or upper class even though you may feel that you belong to the upper middle or middle class in your own society. You are identified as being an elitist; well-educated and having a lot of money. You need to recognize this.

The second reason is that an awareness of this should help you to better understand the indigenous work force. It is very difficult for a person to get out of the lower class in a two tiered society. One of the ways to move up the ladder, to the next higher class both socially and economically is to make connections in the higher class; at times, connections through you, the foreign manager or supervisor. Why? Because you are perceived as having all the connections—you know all the power brokers.

I was in Santa Cruz, Bolivia in the late 1970s talking to a Bolivian friend of mine and the discussion turned to this topic and his comment to me was that I was one of elitists. I said, "Jose, whatever money I have, I earned. When I went to college I had an athletic scholarship that paid for a part of my tuition and I had a part-time job that paid for the rest. Until I was gainfully employed full-time, I worked every summer since I was 16 years old. I even managed to save up enough money to buy a brand new auto in 1962. I wasn't born with money or an education. And what did Jose think of all of this? He sucked up some more of his *cerveza* and asked me if I could get his cousin a job at the American Embassy. Why? Because according to Jose I knew *everybody* there. I did not even make a dent into the pre-conceived belief that he had about the people I knew or the influence that I had in the American community; or the fact that I worked my ass off for whatever I had.

Once again, be aware of the fact that foreign national employees in the Low Human Development (LHD) countries have a slim chance of upward mobility. While limited opportunity and chance is certainly viewed as a fault by some in any country, it is definitely more pronounced in LHD countries. This may affect their attitude towards you; the perceived elitist, upper-class manager which in turn could also have an impact on their work habits in the work place.

Somewhat related to this is the ominous, and obvious *brain drain* that you will undoubtedly hear about; those well-educated citizens who see more opportunity and chances for advancement and recognition and compensation in High Human Development countries. This unfortunate occurrence exists in far too many countries.

And this is spilling over into the trades group as well. There are literally thousands of Bolivian masons, plumbers, electricians, etcetera who have migrated to Spain. Plus look at immigration statistics in other European High Human Development countries and you will see the same pattern emerging.

Tony Blair, ex-Prime Minister of England is credited with saying:

> "*A simple way to take measure of a country is to look at how many want in . . . and how many want out.*"

While the following may sound a bit outdated it is still worth mentioning. Possibly complicating this issue may be considerations in some countries were some people may still have feelings of class based on country specific ethnicities/mores such as the Indian Caste System or the Japanese feudal class system. To touch briefly on this in the Indian system the four primary castes are: *Brahmins* or Hindu priests and teachers; *Kshatriyas*, the kings and warriors; *Vaisyas*, the farmers, merchants and skilled artisans; and *Shudras*, the tenant farmers, servants and laborers. Below these are the "untouchables" or *dalits* or *harijans* who do the unclean jobs such as tanning leather, collecting garbage, butchering, etc. This system came out of the Hindu belief of reincarnation.

Under the feudal Japanese system, the four classes are: Samurai or warriors; Farmers, Artisans; and Merchants. Below these were the *burakumin* and *hinin* who performed the same type of work as their Indian counterpart "untouchables" did. This system came out of Confucian philosophy, rather than religion.

Over the year's education, job availability and general acceptance of people have allowed for more upward mobility, especially for women in both of these systems. Again, in all probability this may not be an issue or concern in your work environment but something to keep in mind none-the-less.

Be Aware of the Class Structure in the Host Country.

CULTURE AND TRADITION:

A more effective manager relishes the thought of learning about the culture and traditions in the host country.

I am sure that someone could have written a whole book about this. Maybe someone already has. This is probably one of the most basic awareness elements to identify but one that is too often overlooked.

Why? One reason is that many people do not want to lose their own identity or roots. We would like to act and operate like we would back home. The U.S. Government is so concerned about this that it budgets (or at least it did) millions of dollars to ensure that USG foreign service employees working overseas can "readjust" back to life in the United States when they return home.

Some might ask if this is really necessary. In addition to having access to a post or regional counselor, employees and their families can return to the United States, at USG expense once each year; the first year for Rest and Recuperation (R & R) and the second year for Home Leave. Most employees also return to the U.S. for conferences, meetings or seminars. To a number of people, the "return to readjust" may sound like over-compensation to employees who chose this career path and way of life.

Notwithstanding the above there can be changes that one might see when he/she gets back home or revisits the neighborhood: new buildings, streets or neighbors to name a few. One the lighter side, on one of my trips back to the "hood" in Connecticut I happened to use the restroom where I saw that one of the urinals was significantly closer to the floor than the others.

When I returned to Cairo and mentioned this at a party, before I could even finish the thought one of the ladies blurted out that the lower one was for the *little boys*. My reply—"I thought it was for the real men; I get tired of standing on my toes." The comments of "yeah, right" resonated throughout the group and her beet red face was accompanied by a good laugh by everyone.

The private sector is not altogether that different. Most companies offer some sort of R & R incentive, especially to employees working in a Low Human Development country. You may likewise have an option of returning to your home country or to some other country close to where you are working for this R&R.

Another factor that hinders one's awareness of cultural differences is the fact that people tend to feel more comfortable with their own countrymen. Consequently, the American Community Center or the British Women's Club become quite popular.

The positives of schooling for children in an overseas environment and attending international schools like the American Cooperative School, the French School, a British School or the German School may also contribute to ones' cultural isolation. Incidentally, I am not criticizing this. Schools, churches and community specific activities have a very important role to play in the life of the overseas employee. How they impact on your way of life in the foreign country is your choice.

Another difficulty with becoming aware of cultural differences is that there are so many that we tend not to focus on, or become aware of any. Culture, by definition covers the customary beliefs, social forms, and material traits of a racial, religious, or social group. We've said a mouthful here right?

Why should the more effective manager be aware of cultural differences? An awareness of cultural differences is a part of your continuing education of understanding the indigenous work force that you supervise. It also plays an important role in understanding your host country customers and clients and your host country counter-parts, competitors and adversaries. In short, your awareness of culture differences will help you in darn near every phase of your operation; from policy setting to negotiations to price setting.

Host country culture issues may have a real impact on the work attitude and ethics in the work environment. They may even impact on the work standards and work quality that you may, or may not be accustomed to. Don't panic. This is one area that goes hand in hand with—patience.

An understanding of cultural differences will help you manage the work force by helping you focus on such things as time management and scheduling. This is similar to understanding religious holidays (discussed earlier) and both may be predicated not only on the traditional yearly calendar but, in the Muslim and Chinese world on the lunar calendar as well.

In the work place; the wearing of different items such as head-covers may be readily apparent. Employees may come in wearing a *yarmulke*, turban, fez, beret, *kufie*, *chira* or whatever.

I previously mentioned fasting so I will not dwell on this. Fasting during the Moslem Ramadan period oftentimes contributes to employee lethargy. Going without solid food or liquids from sun-up to sun-down can be pretty taxing on a person. More so if it falls during the long and intolerably hot summer. Why do I know this? I know it because I partook in Ramadan in each and every year that I was in Cairo. Why—because I wanted to experience firsthand what it was like.

Cultural differences can be seen in your social integration into the community. Most obvious is eating with chopsticks rather than with a fork or spoon.

In India eating with your hand is quite common. The cardinal rule is to use the right hand for eating or receiving food and never the left hand and eat what is nearest to you first. The left hand is considered unclean and is used for cleaning oneself.

In Korea it may be viewed as un-polite to chew food with your mouth closed. Chewing with the mouth open and making all kinds of sounds shows the host or hostess that you are really enjoying the food.

Someone remarked to me that in Cairo you will readily become aware of cultural differences when you see the ninety thousand dollar Mercedes Benz creeping along behind and waiting to pass, the vegetable cart being pulled by one donkey—on a main highway or thoroughfare.

It may be somewhat hard to believe but you see something like this every day. Don't fret; the *boab* will clean the donkey doo off the car's hub caps.

Stretching the point and on an even lighter side, especially for Americans how about seeing women drinking a glass of beer though a straw? The first time I witnessed this as a common practice in restaurants was in the tiny new country of Montenegro. So being a rather naïve foreigner I asked a friend of mine why they did this. I had heard from the old stories that it was easier to get a tad inebriated if you drank "shots" of beer or beer through a straw.

The real reason that he gave me was that it kept the ladies from smearing their lipstick on the glass. It was a win-win situation for the ladies and the barkeeps. For the ladies, it was easier to maintain their cherry red lips and for the bar-keep, no lipstick smudges to clean off the glasses. Now I firmly believe that the myth of getting a buzz on if you drink beer through a straw was debunked. I very seldom saw a blitzed young lady being obnoxious or making an ass of herself after imbibing in beer or two or three through a straw.

And don't forget to consider differences within the country that you are working. There are significant differences in Bolivia between the various departments; for example La Paz, Santa Cruz, Potosi and Tarija. Upper Egypt and Lower Egypt also come to mind as does the northern part of India and the southern part of that country.

Closely related to this is the introduction of new traditions that may come from other countries. A good example of this in Bolivia is the celebration of Halloween. This was originally celebrated primarily by Americans on 31 October as it is in the United States, Canada, Ireland and the United Kingdom. While today it is largely a secular celebration it has its roots in the Celtic festival of Samhain and the Christian holiday All Saints Day. Samhain was the thin border between the lighter half of the year and the darker half of the year. This was a time when both harmless and evil spirits could pass through from the Otherworld and into this world. The wearing of masks and costumes was thought to ward off the evil spirits.

Bolivians have a long tradition of celebrating the "Day of the Dead." This holiday focuses on family and friends gathering to pray for and to remember family and friends who have died. While scholars trace the origins of this modern holiday back to an Aztec festival dedicated to the goddess Mictecacihuatl, this celebration occurs on 2 November in connection with the Catholic holidays of All Saints' Day (1 November) and All Souls' Day (2 November). Most of the celebrations and remembrances occur at gravesites and include building private alters honoring the departed using sugar skulls and offering food and drink to them.

Herein lays the problem. Because the "Day of the Dead" occurs shortly after Halloween, it is now sometimes thought to be a similar holiday. In reality, the two have very little in common. However, some old timers see Halloween as eventually surpassing and supplanting the "Day of the Dead" as the more *traditional* holiday in Bolivia that will be celebrated during this period. The "Day of the Dead" will fade away into oblivion according to these doomsayers; which, if this truly happens will be most unfortunate as tradition gives us a link to the past. It also gives us a feeling that we are a part of something larger than ourselves.

While touching on this in the preceding three paragraphs but on a more grandiose scale, beyond the scope of this book is the emergence of multicultural societies. This is fast becoming a reality as the world literally becomes smaller and more homogenized as multinational companies expand and countries relax immigration laws. How governments and its citizens react to, adjust to and legislate this phenomenon may be an issue that the more effective manager has to deal with in a foreign country.

Worthy of mentioning again is that if a country's culture and traditions are not valued, the cry of "Yankee go home" addressed to the large multinational corporation or foreign embassy because; "You are only here to rape, pillage, plunder and exploit our mineral resources and the labor force of our poor country" may resonate throughout the real world that you are managing in. Maybe other industrial/investment giants like China, India or Japan should take heed.

Be Aware of Cultural and Traditional Differences in the Host Country.

CULTURAL SENSITIVITY:

A More Effective Manager always gives his attention to "Cultural Sensitivity" in a conscientious manner.

Having discussed cultural differences in the previous discussion topic let me briefly mention cultural sensitivity by re-printing an E-mail that I received from a colleague of mine (Names of individuals, except mine deleted of course). I believe that this puts the exclamation point on the broad issue of cultural awareness.

To further set the stage, I believe that everyone needs to remind themselves that they are effective managers. One of the ways I reinforce this is to hang up on the wall in my office some of my most memorable recognition awards and personal items that attest to this. Therefore, I tacked the following email on my office wall in Cairo in where I thought was a very inconspicuous place.

> *"Dave—How the heck are you? How's life in the land of the towel heads? (was that culturally insensitive?). Anyway, sorry it took me so long to send you greetings, but it's been hell around here . . . (Name deleted) left last Friday and we won't have the new person on board for a couple of weeks, and someone left this incredibly hellacious report for me to do (I'll get you for this, Korponai). Other than that, everything is great!*
>
> *Finally, I was very sad we didn't have time to have a last chat before you left. I wanted to tell you how glad I was that we had some months together so I could learn a few things from you about being a manager and also about life. You've got an approach to people and to life that I am trying hard to achieve. Anyway, I hope all is well there. Drop me a line and let me know how you're doing. Cheers."*

My boss came in, read the above and recommended that I find a more appropriate place to hang it as the comment ". . . land of the towel heads?" reflected "Cultural Insensitivity." And, he was right. Quite frankly, I never gave a thought to the fact that anyone would walk behind my desk and read an 8 point size font email.

Be Aware of the Meaning of Cultural Sensitivity.

FAMILY AND WOMEN:

A More Effective Manager appreciates the effect that family and women could have in the work place.

Should this be one of your reality tests?

Let's take a look at family first. In the United States as an example, families are viewed as being very mobile and not very close. Latin families are seen as being very close knit. Northern European and Scandinavian families, with maybe the exception of the Germans are viewed as being close, yet very permissive. Oriental families are viewed as being very demanding and stern.

Some of these characteristics may flow into the work place. It is not uncommon in Egypt for a local employee to request time off to take his second or third cousin to the dentist. Find out about the role that the family plays in the country or region that you will be working in. Awareness of this beforehand will enable you to have a better understanding of the indigenous work force that you manage.

A woman's role in some countries is an exceptionally sensitive issue. You may have heard that in some Muslin countries women must walk three paces behind the man. Or in Saudi Arabia women must wear veils when they are outside of the house, at least within their country. In some countries they are not allowed to drive.

Notwithstanding that woman's rights may be further along in Western cultures, don't fool yourself into believing that the beliefs mentioned above are held any less strongly than beliefs concerning women's rights may be held by you.

You must learn how to walk before you can run, right? Change takes time. If you try to impost your cultural ideals on someone else you will be viewed as just a dictatorial manager who is insensitive to host county culture—the "Ugly American" image will begin to show.

Any change you want to bring about in the work place must consider host country customs and traditions and must be brought about in a planned, gradual manner. From my first book, remember, "It May Not Be Right, But That's The Way It Is."

Tread very carefully in this area, especially when it involves you as the manager or supervisor. In some countries that may be considered more male dominant, make every effort to be fair regardless of gender, especially when it comes to promoting someone.

On the lighter side—I read that in a Chicago, Illinois suburban area several years ago a male applicant was suing HOOTERS for not replying to his application for employment. HOOTERS as some of you may know, employees scantily clothed females for high visible positions such as bartending, hosting, and waiting on tables. The roles that the guys get to play are that of short order cooks or backstage washing dishes and taking out the garbage. Hey, who wants to order something from a short, bald-headed, over-weight male dude in pink tights anyway?

A law-suit may not result in your overseas work environment because of a perceived or a real hiring/promotion sexual discrimination incident; but, be forewarned, the more effective manager must be sensitive to the role that women play in not only their own country but even more-so in the host country culture and work place.

For those of you who may be assigned to a position in your company in the United States, woman there are many times often perceived as being aggressive, insensitive, workaholics and overly protective of their turf in the work environment. They may even think of themselves as being on the fast track and untouchable at times.

Be Aware of Employee Family and Women Influences in the Workplace and Society in General.

THE *"Mañana"* SYNDROME:
A More Effective Manger adjusts to the "Mañana" syndrome.

Mañana for those of you who may not know means "Tomorrow" in Spanish. The *Mañana* Syndrome is simply based on the principle that, "Why do today, what you can do tomorrow."

It can be extremely frustrating at first, especially for those of you who will be working in a Spanish speaking Low Human Development country for the first time.

When I decided to return to Bolivia in late 1978, my friends all asked what I would be doing in Bolivia. I told them that the first thing that I would do was to learn how to walk—Meaning that I knew that the *pace* in Bolivia was somewhat slower than that in the United States.

This may be true in the host country work environment in both the private and public sectors. Why? I really don't have an answer to this other than there are probably several factors to consider. Among them are low wages; why bust your back or other parts of your body for three dollars a day? and working conditions; Why bust your back, or other parts of your body working in a pig sty?

To stray a bit, the climate may be a consideration in some countries. It gets to be 120 degrees Fahrenheit in the shade in the Sudan in the summertime and not much cooler in the wintertime.

If it's the *Mañana* syndrome in Latin America it's the *In Sha Allah* syndrome in Egypt. *In Sha Allah* means "God willing" or "If it is God's will" in Arabic. That's right; in many work environments this is construed to mean that it could be *longer* than *mañana*! You left a slow paced work environment in Bolivia for an even slower paced work environment in Egypt.

How will the knowledge of the *Mañana* syndrome help you to become a more effective manager? One important thing that this knowledge will do for you is to help you to focus on the importance of time management in the work environment. Effective use of time assists in keeping everyone out of the stress quadrant. It will also help you to prioritize tasks. This of course affects many aspects in the work environment from employee performance and morale to meeting deadlines.

Developing a feeling for the pace in the work environment is not that difficult. It will also help you to get to know the personnel whom you have direct supervision over. Identify the self-starter for example.

The other important thing that you will get out of this knowledge is your own peace of mind. When in Rome, do as the Romans do. When in Egypt, do as the Egyptians do. A more effective manager adjusts to the pace in the work environment while at the same time getting the most out of the people whom he supervises.

Be Aware of the Mañana Syndrome and Its Effect on Workforce Planning.

DRIVING MISS DAISY:

A More Effective Manager should become observant of indigenous habitant driving habits.

Right! How in a million years is your knowledge of host country driving habits going to help you adapt and to become a more effective manager? Because it will help you to better understand the people and the culture that you are working in.

An executive I know recently mentioned to me that you can tell the degree of a country's development by the driving habits of its people. How's that? The less respect that people have for traffic laws, the lesser developed the country. Maybe this is a little unsophisticated but, a theory none-the-less.

Let me give you some examples of this and you can judge for yourself. The third day that I was in Egypt I was a passenger in a vehicle being driven by one of our drivers. He stopped at a red light, and turned right at the intersection. I said, "You can make a right hand turn on red just like you can in the United States." He looked at me and said, "Mister David, you can make right turn on red, go straight on red or make left turn on red. You can do anything you want on red"! And do you know what? He was right on target. If there is little or no risk involved, the cars behind you are honking their horns like crazy if you stay stopped at a red light.

Egypt again—I am in a taxi with two other Americans. We are being driven down a one-way street and here comes someone driving *up* the one-way street. Very few drivers are blowing their horns but are still skillfully moving out of the way. Our taxi driver looks at me and says, "Him very brave man". He didn't say; what a stupid driver or what a crazy f_%*ing idiot. He said, "Him very brave man"! You are admired for having the courage to challenge on-coming traffic in Egypt. I ain't foolin'.

Switch to Almaty, Kazakhstan. Signs indicating pedestrian crossings are on the side of the road about twenty meters from the crosswalk which is further defined by diagonal white stripes painted on the road. I'm being driven home by a company driver at dusk and all of sudden this guy slams on the brakes and I damn near go through the windshield. Why? Some guy had entered the crosswalk with his nose up in the air knowing that Kazak drivers have so much respect for this law that he can literally stroll across the street without a care in the world.

In Bolivia, not too long ago about 98% of the drivers did not drive with headlights on at night. They wanted to save the battery. And, believe me there are some very treacherous roads in Bolivia marked by narrow hair-pin curves, no guard rails and pot holes that could swallow up a semi. Now about 95% of them drive with their headlights *on* at night. It is good to see the results of twenty years of education.

In Kingston, Jamaica it seems that everyone blows their horn for a variety of reasons. To give a pedestrian or another vehicle the right of way, to acknowledge and say "thank you" for giving me the right of way, to say "you're welcome" to the guy you gave the right away to, to "beep beep—move your rear end the light just turned green"!—Beep-beep, beep-beep, beep-beep!

Throw in the mundane irritants such as double parking, blocking an intersection so no one can drive through, having no respect for cars trying to get out of a roundabout, passing in obvious no-passing zones, making a left hand turn from the right lane or running a red light and you see what I mean. And it is not because drivers are ignorant or stupid. It is because they show little respect for traffic laws. Unfortunately, in far too many cases this carries over into their attitude towards other laws.

I bet my bottom dollar that there are hundreds of more scofflaws in Medium and Low Human Development (MHD/LHD) countries than there are in High Human Development countries. And, slipping a traffic policeman a few bucks to keep from being cited for an infraction is not uncommon in MHD and LHD countries. Just think of the lost revenue to the host country government.

We Americans, of course all know that the British drive on the wrong side of the road. Interestingly enough of the roughly 195 countries in the world, 64 drive on the left hand side of the road. That is almost thirty-three percent of the countries in the world. Included in these are; Australia, Bangladesh, Bophuthatswana, Ciskei, India, Kenya, Sikkim, Thailand, Venda and Zimbabwe. It goes from A to Z.

Give yourself more peace of mind in the work environment by knowing a little something about the host country driving habits. The sooner the better I might add.

Be Aware of Driving Habits in the Host Country.

LIGHTING UP:
A More Effective Manager influences smoking habits of the indigenous work force.

I mention this in view of the smoking policies being pushed by the U.S. Government, state and municipal governments and some private American companies as well. Fast food chains like MacDonald and Taco Bell have a No Smoking policy in corporate owned facilities.

You will probably find a more laissez-faire attitude about smoking in most foreign countries, especially in the Low Human Development ones and companies outside of the United States. If you are a strong advocate of a non-smoking policy, be prepared to meet some resistance. Remember, change takes time. If you do decide to institute a NO SMOKING policy in the work environment, have patience, patience and more patience.

Again, the approach you take will be remembered by your staff. It may be the right time to play the "concern for your health" theme. Or, how about adding this subject to the agenda for your next retreat and help educate the entire staff. Will you set up some designated smoking areas for those employees who do not want to quit? If you are an American and try to force a policy on your work force, what is the risk involved pertaining to cultural sensitivity and surfacing the "Ugly American" image?

Will your efforts in this area be seen as being done by someone who cares and is a real people oriented, caring manager? Or, will they be viewed as being done solely for the reason because, "That's the way we do it in Canton, Ohio."

Be Aware of Smoking Habits in the Host Country.

Work Force Planning

LOCALLY EMPLOYED STAFF (INDIGENOUS WORK FORCE):

A More Effective Manager welcomes learning about and putting to good use the talents found in the local manpower work force.

This should be obvious: the selection of local staff is critical. This is true when selecting blue collar workers (skilled, semi-skilled or unskilled), white collared workers or professionals.

Bear in mind that especially in Low Human Development and in countries with a high rate of unemployment it is not unusual to hire someone with a professional degree to fill positions that they are over qualified for, at least at the education level. Let me give you some concrete examples.

In USAID/Cairo we had a person with a medical degree who was our expendable supply store keeper. He eventually got a visa to go to the United States and through hard work and perseverance, he is now board certified in, I believe the state of Illinois.

The most sought after Russian language teacher in USAID/Almaty had a degree in Russian literature and languages. While she stayed in her field of linguistics this multi-talented, young woman had other goals and aspirations. She also picked up teaching assignments with international organizations and still found time to follow her passion of writing poetry. Her book of short poems, in the Russian language was recently published in the United States by Trafford Publishing. I will give credit where credit is due and put in a pitch for her. Her name is Svetlana Ni.

Staying in USAID/Almaty, the vibrant and lovely young lady handling the Mission's Human Resources has a degree in Robotic Engineering. Prior to joining USAID she was a project manager for a design team that was tasked with coming up with a better way to move heavy containers within a state owned cement plant. Bottom line; her work load was heavy and her compensation was ultra-light.

Private sector companies and foreign assistance agencies like USAID or Deutsche Gesellschaft fur Internationale Zusammenarbeit (GTZ) or The Japan International Cooperation Agency (JICA) or the World Bank come along with salary offers that are in line with what a person is really worth. It is like an internal "brain drain" within the host country, state-run companies

In USAID/Podgorica the multi-talented person with a degree in civil engineering acted as the Deputy Executive Officer and Supervisory General Services Officer. In addition to this she was an interpreter at high level meetings with USG and Government of Montenegro officials. She was the go-between between American embassy officials and the Mayor of Podgorica during sensitive and critical discussions of property acquisition by the USG and expansion of the existing embassy facilities. She was so good I sometimes wondered why I was needed there.

The senior secretary for S.J. Groves & Sons in La Paz, Bolivia had a degree in economics. She spoke five languages, including Japanese and also did instantaneous interpreting.

Let's get back to a more general discussion. Many professionals and white collar workers in foreign countries, especially those in Medium and Low Human Development countries get all or some of their college undergraduate and graduate work in the High Human Development countries. In Latin American for example, many get their degrees in the United States, Germany, England or Chile. In Africa many get these degrees in any number of European countries.

Much thought should go into the selection of professional staff, white collar workers and consultants. You may feel more comfortable with someone who was educated in your home country not only because of the education they received, but you may be able to communicate with them better because of the commonality of the language.

Selection of blue collared workers should be done just as carefully as selecting a professional. While they may not have a strong academic background, their training and experience in the trades must be looked at very closely. It may take just as long, in some cases to find and hire a very good auto mechanic or plumber or electrician as it is to find and hire an office manager but, guaranteed it will save you time and money in the long run by lowering personnel turnover.

Your home country embassy may be able to give you leads as to trade schools or training institutions where you may be able to recruit staff from. Don't forget to look to the various chambers of commerce for leads either.

Take a long, hard look at your need for supervisors and the proportion of supervisory staff to employees. What is a good ratio in the country you are working in; one supervisor to seven workers or one supervisor to three workers? How will the local work force accept supervision from a foreigner? Are there country specific ethnic considerations to think about when putting together a new staff or augmenting your current work force?

Do you have to consider support staff? Illustration—In the mining sector, how many support people will you need to support one underground miner? In the government owned mines in Bolivia, the ratio was roughly three support/administrative people to one miner. In the private sector it was roughly one to one.

Identify your real staffing needs. Whatever you do, do not fall into the trap of trying to mirror your staffing pattern or needs after similar operations in your home country. Knowledge of the indigenous manpower pool will allow you to hire a quality staff that will make your overseas managing less difficult.

While you are at it, find out about the local compensation plan. Maternity leave works like this in Kazakhstan for example. Picture a three year block of time beginning the day the baby is born. The first four months the mother can take off with full pay. She can then use all of her accrued vacation and sick leave and receive full pay. After that if she decides to take off additional time or leave without pay her position is held open for her for the remaining time that she takes off up the end of the three year period.

Be Aware of the Potential of Locally Employed Staff.

LOCALLY EMPLOYED STAFF INITIATIVE/DEVELOPMENT:
A More Effective Manager is patient with the development of foreign national employees.

I have found that in too many instances foreign national employees display too little initiative. There are exceptions of course and I'll note them below. The qualifiers here are the level of the position, the education level of the employee and the type of position that the employee occupies.

You should be aware of this because it may have an impact on your short and long range planning. Depending on the management situation you are in, ask such questions and decide, "Who can take up the slack when you are out of the office or the shop? "Who can get things done with little or no supervision"? "Who might be a candidate to replace you"?

Case in point: When I was the Supervisory General Services Officer (S/GSO) in USAID/Bolivia I saw, in my opinion management potential in our Motor Pool dispatcher. However, his English language skills were very poor. So, with some prompting and prodding he engaged in some on-line English language courses. Shortly after I left the Mission he became, you guessed it—the S/GSO.

What I saw this in this young man was summed up very nicely by Henry David Thoreau when he said:

"It's not what you look at that matters, it's what you see."

What I saw was management potential. Now he not only supervises the motor pool (dispatching and vehicle maintenance) but the warehousing operation, customs and shipping and a residential housing program.

In the 36 plus years that I have been managing in the overseas environment, I believe that the major stumbling block in indigenous hire initiative is fear of losing their job if they make a mistake, or a *bad* recommendation, or a *bad* decision (if they are in a decision making position).

I was discussing this several years ago with my sister-in-law who is aggressive, bright, very attractive and Bolivian. With an MBA from Boston University she was a bank officer with the First National Bank of Boston (FNBB) in La Paz, Bolivia. When the bank closed its' operations there she assumed the position of the financial manager for Lufthansa in La Paz. When Lufthansa regionalized and moved their main office to Lima, Peru and right sized their operation in Bolivia, she took over their cargo operation in La Paz. And at the same time she started her own travel company.

Prior to starting with the FNBB she used her own initiative to get an advanced degree. She also recognized the importance of foreign investment in Bolivia and the role that foreign companies and investors had to play in the development process; in this case the FNBB. Again using her own initiative she networked her way into management positions within the bank branch office in La Paz.

Her attitude with both the FNBB and Lufthansa when they terminated their operations in Bolivia was one of, "Piss on 'em, I'll be here longer than they will." And, she was right.

A more effective manager must have the patience to develop Locally Employed Staff (LES) to assume greater responsibilities in the company or organization. In the private sector this is imperative.

I was told by an executive of Freeport-McRowan, a large and very successful mining company that their company policy is to turn over nearly the entire foreign project to foreign national management within 5-8 years of the project; that is, from exploration through mobilization to production. I believe that the reason for this may be twofold: 1. to eliminate the "Ugly American" image; and, 2. it is more cost effective in the long run. Staff from the home office still visit, give advice and assist in the project, on a limited and as needed basis.

The development of the indigenous work-force, to include technical training and training in management skills contributes to the success of this policy. A more effective manager must initiate, and keep the momentum of educating LES a top priority in the work environment. This will stimulate deep thought and open dialog amongst employees and serve as a vehicle to improve operations.

In some work arenas, including the US Government the action of delegating authority is empowerment. This not only implies but demands that the individual empowered must be able to use their own initiative.

Speaking of empowerment I attended a conference for Department of State (DOS) Management Officer's for the overseas bureau that I was working in at the time. One of the senior executives from the bureau was down from Washington, D.C. for the conference. He said unequivocally and on more than one occasion that the USAID and the Department of Defense were light years ahead of the DOS when it came to understanding the concept of empowerment of Locally Employed Staff and implementing this invaluable management tool. Why? One reason, in my opinion is the reluctance that many American government employees have to give up power and control. And this was borne out by the many comments made by the people at the conference.

Added to the reluctance of a supervisor to relinquish power and control you have to factor in the reluctance of the home office to give up power and control. This was something that Freeport-McRowan dealt with and blended in very nicely with their overseas operations.

The bottom line—Do not underestimate Locally Employed Staff. Do not underestimate their intelligence, their willingness to learn and the patience that they have with you. While LES are being mentored and developed by you, don't miss your opportunity to learn from them. And remember the institutional memory that they bring to the organization.

A more effective manager *must* develop indigenous hire employees and create a work environment where they are not afraid to use their initiative. This, along with empowerment could be a real challenge in some countries.

Empowerment leads to the question of decision making? As Wilfred A. Peterson, author of *The Art of Living* and *The Art of Marriage* said:

> *"Decision is the spark that ignites action. Until a decision is made nothing happens."*

While none of the people whom you manage may be in a position to make a decision if the final choice is yours you should bring your subordinates into the decision making process. That's right—don't forget that *decision making is a process* and it is all about the team effort.

Be Aware of the Value Gained in Developing Locally Employed Staff.

EX-PATRIOTS (Ex-Pats) IN THE HOST COUNTRY:

A More Effective Manager taps into the manpower pool of ex-patriots residing in a host country.

Simply defined an ex-patriot is someone who withdraws himself from his residence or allegiance to his native country. Speaking from some knowledge of this on the American side of the fence one will find a large number of American ex-patriots living in such countries as Costa Rica, Germany or Japan. Others of wanderlust are scattered around the globe and like myself, wind up in places like Bolivia, Egypt, Thailand or wherever.

Ex-pats are normally an excellent source of information about the host country. This could include not only a hands-on assessment of the business climate but the political climate in the country as well. As mentioned, some were a reference source for me when I wrote my thesis that led to a Master's Degree in Business Management. There is nothing wrong with tapping into other people's knowledge of and experiences in the host country. Ask them what they like, or dislike about the country and its' people. And don't forget the possible contacts that they may already have in country; contacts that you may be able to tap into

And, how about using them as a part of your manpower pool? In addition to a common language you may find one or two that have skill sets that will fit nicely into your scheme of things. I mentioned being hired by the American company, S.J. Groves & Sons when I went back to Bolivia in the late 1970s. Commonly referred to as a "resident hire" most often it is fairly easy to hire someone from this group. If on a temporary basis, you may not have to go through the process of verifying work permits either. You can use this manpower pool as a source to provide surge coverage. Keep their names on file to stock the bullpen so to speak.

Working example: While in Cairo with USAID, and looking at reorganizing our warehousing operation we identified a real need for an American supervisor at the warehouse. The importance of housing, which also included providing furniture and furnishings for maintaining and improving employee morale (and, hopefully increased productivity) was important to the Mission. The hiring of an American, who was residing in Cairo at the time allowed for better communication with employee spouses. This, coupled with his insight to expand a reupholstering program that saved the United States Government thousands of dollars annually had a very positive effect on improving employee morale. The fact that he spoke Arabic and had managerial skills second to none translated into a more efficient, cost saving operation.

As a final point, the cost of ex-pat labor will undoubtedly be less expensive than hiring someone off-shore from your own country. In most cases these folks are already established in country, know the ins and outs of working there and have at least a working knowledge of the local language.

We can expand on this a smidgen and include in this group the person in transient as well. For example, someone backpacking through country or in the case of the person hired in Cairo for the warehousing operation, a graduate student who decided to extend his stay in Egypt to learn even more about the country Depending on the country that you are in, this may give you a certain amount of additional comfort and security, which in turn will give you more peace of mind in the work place and to take home with you at night.

Ex-pats may also be a source for social networking. Many times groups trend to stick together because of work relationships. The embassy coterie, the ARAMCO or the Groves group or the teacher's bowling league are a few prime examples of this.

Check out the local bowling alley or golf course or *gringo* hangouts. For Americans in Cairo it was the Maadi House or the Cairo Rugby Club, in Kiev it was a sports bar named Planet Sport, in Saigon the rooftop bar at the Rex Hotel was the in place, in Kingston the Sweetwood Jerk Joint across from the Hotel Courtleigh was a good place to meet ex-pats, in La Paz, Bolivia Reinke Fuchs and La Campana had the upper hand and in Almaty, Mad Murphy's played to the ex-pat community.

Focusing on the business side, try to identify other companies from your country operating in the host country or posting an interest in doing so. Stop by your embassy's commercial office and get a current listing of companies operating there. A visit to the Chamber of Commerce may be in order. Doing so may not only expand your knowledge of the business community but lead to connections to a larger ex-pat community.

Let me wrap this up with this little ditty I recently received from one of my friends. It was entitled *Expats Ten Commandants.*

1. *Thou shalt not expect to find things as thou hast them at home for verily thou shall hadth left home to explore different things.*

2. *Thou shalt not take anything too seriously, for a care-free mind is essential for a healthy body.*

3. *Thou shalt not let other expats get upon thy nerves, for one or both of you are likely to be transferred soon anyway.*

4. *Thou shalt refrain from acting exceedingly high and mighty, for thou art the same person you were before you had a cleaning lady, maids and/or drivers.*

5. *Thou shalt not buy everything you seeth; thou already hast a house full of things stored in your home country.*

6. *Thou shalt not sit around and mope and feel unwanted or unskilled; there art many people and organizations that would be grateful for your donations of time and energy.*

7. *Thou shalt not worry, for he that worrieth hath no pleasure—and few things are ever truly fatal.*

8. *When in Rome. Thou shalt be prepared to do somewhat as the Romans do.*

9. *Thou shalt not judge the people of the country by the one person who has given thee trouble.*

10. *Remember that thou art a guest in a foreign land, and he who treateth his host with respect shall be honored.*

Be Aware of the Manpower Pool of Ex-patriots in the Host Country.

THIRD COUNTRY NATIONALS (TCNs):

A More Effective Manager takes advantage of Third Country National (TCN) resources.

As previously defined, a Third Country National (TCN) is an employee with a citizenship from a country other than that of the host country or the home country of the employing company/Agency; for example a Korean citizen working for an American company in Saudi Arabia. A large portion of the domestic help in Egypt is Filipino or Asian while many of the construction laborers in Saudi Arabia are Korean.

Depending on the country that you are in, this human resource area can prove to be a very valuable source of sometimes scare human resources.

The TCN employee may provide the bridge that you need in your organization at mid-level management. You may find that some TCNs have lived in a host country for a long time. I know several British citizens in this category working for American companies in Bolivia, in senior level management positions. There are also a good number of Brits in Jamaica and I would guess in a number of former British colonies. You may want to tap into these kinds of people for short-term employment as consultants or trainers for instance.

One of the difficulties that you will face however, may be the acceptance of the TCN by your host country hired staff. The perception, whether real or not that you are taking a job away from the local labor force will surface. How you handle this is another matter. This could be a very sensitive issue depending on the country that you are working in, the type or positions that you are hiring a TCN to fill and the number that you are employing.

Two other issues that come to mind and need to be dealt with are salary structure/benefits and host country work permits. Are salary/benefits somewhere between that of locally employed staff and an off-shore home country hired employee? It would be prudent to check with your local attorney regarding eligibility of a TCN to work in the host country. Some countries have very strict and time sensitive labor restrictions.

And don't forget that this group of employees and their family members will, in all probability also need your administrative and logistical support. About a month or so after I arrived in Cairo we had a newcomer's welcome brunch. Invitations were normally extended to the new American employees and their family members. This particular session was also attended by several newly hired TCN employees and their families. The Mission Director spent about five minutes stressing how important housing matters were to him and his interest in that area. He also went on to say that if anyone felt that they were not getting adequate support in this area that he wanted to know about it. As the Supervisory General Services Officer this was my area of responsibility. When I introduced myself my comment was that I also wanted to know if anyone was displeased with services in this area but—I wanted to know about it *before* the Mission Director. All I asked for was the first shot at resolving and fixing their problems, be they real or perceived.

Just this little comment showed that I cared and had an interest in the well-being of not only the American employees but the TCN employees as well. When the word of my comment spread throughout the mission, my stock rose significantly.

At any rate, keep an open mind when it comes to the composition of your work force.

Be Aware of the TCN Manpower Pool Both Within, and Outside of the Host Country.

DIVERSE WORK FORCE:
A More Effective Manager eagerly accepts the challenge of managing a diverse workforce.

While I discussed host country indigenous, expatriate, and third country national hiring and staffing in separate awareness elements, let's try to put all of this together. How you meld this group into an efficient, effective and well-functioning staff will test all of your management skills and abilities.

Putting together and managing a multi-national workforce is both exciting and challenging. The exchange of culture is fascinating alone. Add to this such considerations as: work attitudes (Someone from the *Mañana, mañana* zone on the same team as someone on the fast track who wanted to get things done on today's calendar, yesterday; habits (A two hour versus a 30 minute lunch break?); acceptance of a *foreigner* as a supervisor or manager; scheduling (Do Christians and Jews get both Christmas and Yom Kippur off?); dress codes (Can the Indian wear his flowing sari in the workplace? Maybe not in a machine shop.); and, eating habits (Do you have a cafeteria, Kosher foods for Jews, non-pork choices for the Muslims? Utensils for those not used to eating with their fingers) and you can see how this area can be challenging as well.

The development of teamwork can be challenging also. Can this work force work together—Any animosities between the Irishman and the Englishman? How about the ex-pat who was in a management position and now is being supervised by a host country foreign national?

I have found that an often underutilized source of achieving a sense of teamwork in the office, section or company is the retreat. Bringing people together in an out of office environment to discuss work related issues will inevitably lead to a more productive and healthier work environment in the long run. And, I'd bet my last dollar that you will see immediate, positive results.

The rewards of managing a multi-national workforce and getting multi-national synergism far outweigh the extra time and efforts that may be involved. Think of the HOMEDICS tagline for its line of Bob Marley products:

"Working together for a better world."

The U.S. Government throws into the mix several categories of employees. In addition to an assorted group of employees that most likely will include local Foreign Service Nationals/Cooperating Country Nationals and could include third country foreign nationals there are different classifications of American employees. Included in this group are U.S. Direct Hires, Eligible Family Members, U.S. Personal Service Contractors and Recalled Retirees.

I have always had a tremendous amount of respect and admiration for the USAID Mission Director who is able to get the most out of such a diverse group of employees. Their people managing skills coupled with program management and implementation are certainly extraordinary. Throw into this caldron the uncertainty of Washington political decisions coming down the road and normal inter-Agency in-fighting and money grabbing. The reality of managing in an environment where government is becoming more centralized and the leadership at the apex is becoming even more control happy and you can see where it takes an exceptional person to fill this role.

I have found that the very best directors, the ones who keep the Mission from becoming a dysfunctional unit are the ones who realize that it is not only the intellectual cream at the top of this diverse group that keeps things together. They understand and acknowledge that the people who deal with the everyday nitty-gritty and at times mundane tasks can make or break someone's reputation or career just as easily as the over-achiever or person on the fast-track; especially if the person is out for his own personal gain.

When dealing with your most precious resource, people the bottom-line, as in most cases is to be a good listener and to treat them fairly. In my experience the best way to get people to do things that they would not normally do is to develop an atmosphere that they *work with* you and *not for* you.

Be Aware of the Dynamics of Your Diverse Workforce.

TRAINING AND RETENTION:
A More Effective Manger trains and retains employees.

While I may have touched upon this in another awareness element, this topic deserves special attention.

I mentioned in my first book that your most precious resource is people. I have found out over the years that you can better retain employees if you develop a formal staff training program. The risk of them leaving and finding another job once they are trained is minimal. I strongly believe that the reason for this is that it shows that you care about people and this leads to employee loyalty to you and to your company.

While training and retention is important in any work environment, it is even more important to recognize its value in an overseas location. For one reason, the skill bases in the local manpower pool may not be at the level that you want or desire. You may also have to consider some training in areas that require interaction with your home office. Perhaps training in more advanced, or company specific software programs for reporting purposes is in order.

A more effective manager must take a look at all employee training needs and at the training resources that are available to him. Some of the needs may be job related; for example increasing computer skills to keep abreast with competitors in the industry or business. When S.J. Groves & Sons brought into Bolivia the first Caterpillar D-9 tractors, you got it, no qualified local operators to run them. Solution—Set up an in-house, company staffed training program.

How about the need to train automotive mechanics in electronic diagnostic techniques? When I was in Egypt we sent our motor pool supervisor who was also a certified and skilled mechanic to the General Motor training facility in the United States for this purpose.

What I mentioned in the previous paragraph was related to technical skills. How about management skills or decision making skills? Do you feel confident that the person whom you leave in charge while you are on vacation is skilled enough in these areas? Is this a part of your one-on-one mentoring of staff? And don't forget that there are any number of highly sought after consulting companies out there who offer management skill courses. They may be a bit pricey but a training source nonetheless.

I already mentioned the philosophy of Freeport-McRowan to turn the operation over to Cooperating Country National staff. Again, the success of this philosophy is based on the selection, training, and retention of the indigenous work force. This may include changing work habits and attitudes and developing teamwork or management skills among the host country staff. Technical training in the operation of mining equipment may be called for. Training at the home office to go over areas such as company specific computer programs or other data collection programs pertaining to work in progress or production schedules may be warranted.

W. Edward Deming, the father of Total Quality Management (TQM) said:

"Learning is not compulsory, neither is survival."

Let me put this to rest by mentioning a company oriented specific end result that could come about because of an active, board based training program. Through this employees will learn that the organization cares about its employees which will undoubtedly help ensure its *survival* in the fast paced, ever changing and highly competitive international arena.

Be Aware of the Need for Employee Training and Retention.

General Work Environment

THE GIFT FROM JUAN:
A More Effective Manager is sensitive about receiving gifts or gratuities.

This is an area that involves cultural awareness. Outside of the work environment and in some cultures people may be extremely generous in their ways. You will hear many stories of this. In Saudi Arabia for example if you admire a host's painting and show that admiration very strongly and outwardly the host may take it down from the wall and give it to you. What's a few thousand dollars to an oil rich Saudi right?

This becomes even more sensitive in the work environment. Some people, especially those in Low Human Development countries might give you a gift in the hopes of receiving one of greater value. Or, they may give you a gift in the hopes that you will do them a favor. Like what?—A recommendation for that visa to the good old U. S. of A. for one. You may be asked to be a witness at someone's wedding or a Godfather to someone's son.

The rule of thumb should be to tactfully refuse all gifts. Use common sense. The nickel and dime promotional gift such as a desk calendar from one of the local travel agencies is no big deal. A more effective manger knows when to say "no" and also how to keep the "yes" answer from being construed as preferential treatment by the rest of the work force. The common way in Egypt to politely say "no" is to say "yes" three times then do nothing. The person by then should have gotten the message.

Respect for each other's holidays may involve an exchange of gifts. Christmas is a good example of this. One good way to handle this in the work environment is to set a maximum dollar amount that one can spend on a gift.

The important thing here is not to get yourself into a situation that can be construed by others that your acceptance of a gift will result in a favor, or is given in return of a favor. This has to be avoided at all times.

Some employees may place an even greater emphasis on developing a personal relationship rather than a professional relationship in the work environment. This could be a very sensitive area that deserves your special attention. There is nothing that prohibits anyone from forming friendships in the office or shop. What is damaging is the perception that this friendship will lead to faster employee promotions and upward mobility in the company or other types of favoritism. The promotion of your best indigenous friend over someone else who may be more qualified? How about dating your secretary or Spanish teacher? Get the picture? Is the risk worth taking?

Be Aware of, and Wary of the Gift from Juan.

BUSINESS AND PERSONAL RELATIONSHIPS:
A More Effective Manager distinguishes the differences between business and personal relationships.

I have seen that too many times in the general overseas work environment business relationships are built more on friendship than anything else, including competence.

In some countries it's an attitude predicated on the fact that of you have to like someone or know someone before you can do business with him. You conduct business with your friend before you would with someone you don't know. This could develop more into issues related to outside activities.

Depending on the size and structure of your organization one major area that can be affected lies in personnel. Let me give you the following concrete example. The Bolivian employee, who was hired to manage and oversee the hiring of local employees for S.J. Groves & Sons in Bolivia, during the mobilization phase, hired the majority of workers from the Department of Cochabamba region of the country even though the project was in the Department of La Paz. Why? The guy was from Cochabamba. He was a Cochabambino who used his fellow Cochabambino networking to hire employees. Nepotism; i.e. favoritism based on kinship was not found in this case but it is also something that needs to be watched out for.

The above example certainly gives the appearance of partiality right? The result was animosity that led to employee morale problems.

Let's stay with the same company and project and focus in on two more touchy allegations. The first was that the person hired to procure foodstuffs for the mess hall (which at one time served three meals a day to 300 plus employees) was making bulk purchases mostly from his relatives. The second was that the person charged to purchase expendable supplies was buying mostly from the hardware store managed by his old high school crony. The allegations that both men were getting kickbacks proved wrong in both cases, but the perception lingered on nonetheless.

I repeat: A personal relationship that may develop in the work environment is another area that can get a bit dicey and become sensitive. A more effective manger must be wary of personal relationships that may be developing here; especially those that could lead to morale problems. Just as he does outside of the organization he may want to develop personal relationships with the staff who are his coworkers. There is nothing wrong with developing a more personal relationship with a colleague. But, keep it professional within the confines of the work environment.

The main thing here is that you must do everything that you can to be viewed as a *fair* manager and person to work with and to do business with. As a foreigner you will be constantly under the microscope when it comes to your dealings with and relationships with your local hire employees and people who you conduct business with. Do not be intimidated by this. You do have a private life to go along with your professional one.

Be Aware of the Import to Sometimes Keep Distance Between Business and Personal Relationships.

REALITY TEST:
A More Effective Manager develops his own reality tests.

By this I mean test answers to your questions. Is the answer based on what someone *thinks* you want to hear, or is it an answer based on a real set of circumstances or principles.

This pops up a lot when trying to deal with suspense dates or deadlines. Ask yourself, "Can it really be done in five days"? Avoid questions to your subordinates along the lines of; "Can this be done in five days"? or "Will this be ready by Friday"? The answers to these questions in many overseas locations will almost always be an unqualified "Yes boss, if you say so"!

The road construction contract that S.J. Groves & Sons had with the Government of Bolivia (GOB) was let in mid-1977. The GOB established critical path time frame was six months for mobilization and two years to complete the construction. If this were met the project would have been completed in late 1979 or early 1980. Here comes the reality issue. Mobilization was completed almost on schedule. The construction was concluded in mid-1982. Project closure activities, to include demobilization and recovering monies due from the GOB was finished in late 1984.

Looking back in this case, some reality questions that could have been asked should have been related to the role of the consulting engineering company. While a basic design existed, in reality the construction plans were given piecemeal to the Contractor. Furthermore, there was no sequential, consecutive receipt of plans. For example plans were received to construct a section of the road between kilometer 23.4 and 28.8, then kilometer 34.0 to 35.8 and then kilometer 18.7 to 20.0. This necessitated using multiple pioneering and drill and blast teams.

Reality questions related to the time to construct nearly 45 kilometers of detours to keep the old road open while constructing the new 48 kilometer road were also lacking. The reason for the inordinate length of the detours was that the new road was being constructed above the old road. Designated dump areas for excavated material sometimes spilled over and covered the old one. Furthermore this road was the lifeline to bring fresh fruits and vegetables from the countryside to the city of La Paz. It had to be kept open.

On a much broader field, at a level of upper management where policy decisions are made one may want to take heed of what Jawaharlal Nehru noted:

> "*The non-recognition of realities naturally leads to artificial policies and programmes.*"

He also said,

> "*A theory must be tempered with reality.*"

How about those reality test questions related to the *quality* of a product or service? Can you really achieve a high quality product not knowing the quality of say, locally purchased materials used in the final product? And, if you have to import materials, how will it affect your production time schedule?

If you are in the export business, have you set up some type of quality control? The recent stories of the Chinese exporting questionable ingredients that are used in the manufacture of vitamins and health supplements sounds like this might just be lacking over there. Plus, on the importer side of this transaction it looks like the tunnel vision concept of "profit at any cost" has once again clouded the need for quality—all at the expense of the consumer.

When the Quinoa Corporation of America tried to export this high protein grain into the United States they faced several problems related to transportation. Poor infrastructure made it difficult to consolidate harvests purchased from the many small growers in the area. The grain was left on the side of the road or in old warehouses until enough could be collected, bagged and shipped to Arica, Chile. Since Bolivia is a landlocked country this delayed shipments to the port of Arica where the loads were then containerized and shipped to Houston, Texas. On several occasions shipments were denied entry into the United States by health inspectors because the grain had rotted due to transportation delays for one reason or another. There was no quality control at the port of Arica that may have caught some of this and stopped shipments to Houston which would have saved the company the cost of ocean freight.

In my first book, some of the awareness elements discussed that related to this area revolved around: Asking Questions; Setting Realistic

Goals and Objectives; and, Establishing Work *Windows* Rather Than Deadlines. Once again, more than one management awareness component will come into play as the more effective manager completes his management puzzle.

Wherever you may be and whatever or whomever it is that you are managing you may want to remember what Devvy Kidd had to say:

> *"Reality is an ugly beast that most people are incapable of facing."*

Be Aware of the Requirement to Develop Reality Tests.

CHARACTERISTICS IN THE WORKPLACE:

A More Effective Manager looks for distinctive elements in the work place.

What are some other employee related characteristics of the work environment that one should be aware of? Some may revolve around employee performance and changes in that performance. As mentioned earlier, in Egypt, a malaise, laid back, almost lackadaisical attitude of some local staff, especially during the month long celebration of Ramadan is in fact a characteristic of the work environment at that time and something to consider.

A few may center on eating habits. If you are in an organization that provides a cafeteria service, you will probably find mostly local fares being served. I mentioned in my first book the Bolivian workers who were used to a breakfast of coffee, soup, bread, and cheese rather that the more traditional American breakfast of cereal, milk, eggs, toast, and fruits. In Jamaica jerk chicken or pork oxtail or pea soup are on the lunch menu practically every day.

A number may be centered on a combination of host country and home country holiday schedules. In most, if not in all overseas locations the USG respects host country holidays. Employees get the traditional ten American holidays off plus host country holidays (no more than ten also). Plan your work schedule and trips accordingly.

If you are involved in employee pay practices, some may revolve around them. In Bolivia, workers are paid twelve monthly salaries plus a Christmas and Patriotic bonus. This is an additional one month salary per bonus (One paid in December and one paid in June). They also get what is called a "profit sharing" bonus which is supposed to be based on a percentage of a company's annual profit. (All companies pay this whether they show a profit or not!). If working in Bolivia, be prepared to pay fifteen salaries to the Foreign Service National staff.

Although somewhat outside of the work place, the attitude of merchants whom you deal with should be considered. In Egypt for example many merchants charge for most items on a principle that the buyer should pay what he can afford, not on what the merchandise is worth. As the wealthy foreign company, sellers may try to charge you more for some items. Be prepared to bargain or maybe even pay a premium price for a hard to find item and don't complain about it. Go with the flow; be flexible but persistent as well.

Be Aware of the Many Characteristics of the Workplace That You Are Managing In.

CHOOSING AND USING THE RIGHT WORDS:

A More Effective Manager chooses and uses the right words in the work environment and in his everyday activities.

Having worked in an overseas environment for over thirty-six years, I am not sure whether or not I have become overly sensitive to this. By using the right words I mean the choosing of the correct words and phrases that fit the situation that you are in and are understood by whomever you are speaking to. Again, this could turn into a culture sensitive area.

A joint program in Bolivia in the 1980s was established by the governments of Bolivia and the United States. This joint venture was aimed at eradicating the coca plant in Bolivia; this is the plant from which cocaine is derived. Understand that even before the cocaine craze the plant was grown mostly in Peru, Bolivia, and Ecuador and used by the local Indians for centuries in holistic cure-alls. *Eradicate* is a very, very very strong word. *Eradicate* a centuries old tradition—probably not. The name was changed to the Coca *reduction* program. At least the name change made the program easier for the indigenous folks to swallow.

In addition, I have found that host country foreign nationals, and I have worked with and supervised them in Germany, Vietnam, Bolivia, Egypt, Kazakhstan, Montenegro, Chile and Jamaica are, generally speaking more sensitive to criticism that is received from a foreign supervisor. Therefore, the manner in which you criticize, or admonish becomes even more important. The effect that this can have on the whole work force must be taken into account (more on criticizing later).

I once attended a Time Management workshop where one of the major themes was learning how to say "No." This was supposed to help you better manage your time and help you to stay out of the stress quadrant. Saying "No", "*Nyet*" or "*Nein*" may in fact be the right word in many instances. Be careful as to how it may be perceived by the foreign national staff that you manage. If it comes across as; No—*Nyet*—*Nein*—Do it my way or else!—You will most likely be putting yourself *into* the stress quadrant.

You might want to keep in mind this anonymous saying:

> "*Our days are happier when we give people a bit of our heart rather than a piece of our mind.*"

Having just focused on choosing and using the right words, you might want to take into account what the Dalai Lama had to offer as one of his Instructions for Life:

> "*Remember that silence is sometimes the best answer.*"

You might want to keep in mind and remember as well the importance to start with something positive even in a negative situation; something that you may be able to build on. We've all heard this comment, or one very similar: "What do you want to hear first, the good news or the bad news"? Usually it's the good news.

Be Aware of the Necessity in Choosing and Using the Right Words Throughout the Day.

CRITICIZING/JUDGING OTHERS:

A More Effective Manager is mindful of the way that he criticizes in the work environment and how he judges others.

This is even more important when criticizing Locally Employed Staff. While we are all sensitive to criticism, I have found that the indigenous employee is even more sensitive to criticism from a foreign manager or supervisor; an outsider. I am sure that a behavioral scientist or sociologist can tell you the reasons why. I can't. But my gut feeling tells me that this is a real issue that a more effective manager should be aware of.

Think about it. Even in your own home country work environment, when a new boss comes on board and tries to offer suggestions or constructive criticism as to improving the way things are being done what are first reactions? "Hell, he doesn't know what he's talking about"! "He hasn't been here long enough to know what's going on"! "It will cost the company more money if we do it his way"!

For whatever reason, this first reaction to criticism, even constructive criticism, especially if it implies changing the way an employee has been doing something for a long time (a change in the paradigm?) is normally negative. This negative reaction is oftentimes perceived by the foreign national employee as a negative reflection on him as a worker and on the performance of his duties. He takes it personal, at times very personal.

Offering criticism calls for choosing the right words. There are other awareness elements that come into play when considering criticism. Patience for one—Have patience and look at other possibilities that may rest before you before criticizing someone or something.

I am not advocating not correcting things that need correcting in the work place or correcting employee habits that are not acceptable to you or to good management principles; chronic tardiness for example. Use common sense management principles: do not criticize an employee in front of his subordinates; avoid the sarcastic remark that hints of cynicism rather than constructive criticism.

Dale Carnegie had strong feelings about criticism and said,

> *"Criticism is dangerous because it wounds a man's precious pride, hurts his sense on importance and arouses his resentment."*

Be firm, but be fair. Think about what effect the criticism will have on the whole work force. Be sensitive and remember that you are dealing with your company's most precious resource; people.

As far as judging others goes, this anonymous poem says it all:

"I was shocked, confused, bewildered
As I entered Heaven's door,
Not by the beauty of it all,
Nor the lights or its decor.

But it was the folks in Heaven
Who made me sputter and gasp—
The thieves, the liars, the sinners,
The alcoholics and the trash.

There stood the kid from seventh grade
Who swiped my lunch money twice.
Next to him was my old neighbor
Who never said anything nice.

Bob, who I always thought
Was rotting away in hell,
Was sitting pretty on cloud nine,
Looking incredibly well.

I nudged Jesus, 'What's the deal?
I would love to hear Your take.
How'd all these sinners get up here?
God must've made a mistake.

'And why is everyone so quiet,
So somber—give me a clue.'
'Hush, child.' He said,
'they're all in shock.
No one thought they'd be seeing you."

The above only addressed criticizing individuals in the work environment. How about criticism of local politics or things like corruption in the host country; to include within government offices? My suggestion would be to keep it out of the work environment and save it for social functions, over a glass of wine with your dinner guest or amongst your peers. Participating in open forum discussions with other counterparts in a more formal, official capacity is the exception.

Be Aware of How, When and Where You Criticize and/or Judge People.

MISTAKES:

A More Effective Manager is understanding of any mistakes made by the people that he supervises.

You will find that you will the need to check more frequently on the work of foreign national employees filling entry level white-collar or blue-collar positions in Medium and Low Human Development (MHD/LHD) countries. Part of this goes back to the education standards that are sub-standard in most host countries that fall into these categories. Sloppy work habits can also be traced to low salaries. Part of it can be traced to the *Mañana* syndrome. Additionally, for whatever the reason, be prepared to hear all types of excuses.

"I didn't make the mistake, the keyboard made the mistake" was often heard in Bolivia. Part of this may be cultural; saving face for example. Admitting to an error could be based on the fear of being fired, right? A salary of two hundred and fifty American dollars per month in some MHD and LHD countries is an enormous amount of money to the local employee.

Check, re-check and correct. You will find that the foreign national employee, in most cases is willing to learn from his mistakes if you, the more effective manager, are willing to take the time to teach and to mentor. Checking on subordinates work does not mean that you do not trust in them, it shows that you care about them and you care about what goes on in the work environment that you manage.

Be mindful of the way that you correct, and where you correct someone. No yelling and screaming in front of others or in open areas is a good rule of thumb. Let us steal a little from Bob Marley. He was not only a great musician and singer but also a philosopher in his own right. Here are two of his thoughts about this subject that, in my opinion are also applicable in the work place:

"The road of life is rocky
And you may stumble too.
So while you point your finger
Someone else is judging you."

And,

"What we really want
Is the right to be right
And the right to be wrong."

I recently heard that on a flight from New York to Los Angeles, California a Boeing 747 aircraft makes 20,000 in-flight corrections. The lesson to take from this is that once you realize that a mistake has been made, take and make immediate corrective action that will keep the operation on a steady course.

Of course the most ideal situation that one can create in a work environment is one where individuals report their own mistakes to a supervisor. You report on yourself! Sounds Utopian, right? If the environment is one that is non-punitive in nature could this work? Some might argue that it would depend on the severity of the gravity of the mistake that is self-reported.

Be Aware of the Need for Open-mindedness When It Comes to Mistakes in the Office or On the Shop Floor.

EMPLOYEE WORK STATEMENTS:
A More Effective Manager develops clear work statements.

While the need to develop Work Statements or Scopes of Work (SOW) is true in any work environment, it is even more important to develop these in an overseas work environment.

Why? One reason that stands out is that it will reduce misunderstandings because of language. Also, clearly defined, functional tasks and responsibilities will result. There will be less of a chance of duplication of efforts amongst employees. A more effective manager should not renege on his responsibility to define roles and to see that each employee that he supervises understands the role that he or she has to play in the scheme of things.

Work statements, or SOWs are basically position job descriptions and are normally a part of the individual employment contract. It is best to have these in writing and acknowledged in writing by the employee. Have one copy in your native language and one in the language of the host country if it will help. As the old saying goes, "Everyone should be singing off of the same sheet of music."

The SOW is the start of documentation should your company go through a reduction-in-force (RIF) or if you decide to release someone for the convenience of the company. Incidentally, this is difficult in some countries. Be prepared to do battle with the Minister of Labor at a moment's notice. The start of an individual personnel file goes right along with this. Develop the scope of work, advertise and recruit, contract and start an employee personnel file and you are in the human resources business.

These may also set the parameters for an employee's performance evaluation. I spent a good deal of time discussing this in my first book but let me briefly mention it again. Try to develop the *whole man* concept of evaluating and the use of 360 degree feedback. Most important, remember that evaluating is an ongoing process. Employees may show hot flashes of greatness followed by longer periods of average performance. So what, everyone may not be on the fast track, or even want to be on it. But nevertheless they are important members of your team.

Be Aware of the Importance To Provide Polished and Clear Work Statements to Employees.

CREATIVITY:

A More Effective Manager is excited about the opportunities to be creative while working abroad and is cognizant of having to meet head-on the resultant risks that may come along with 'thinking outside of the box."

This creativity should be all encompassing: from looking for ways to expedite customs' clearance of imported goods; to finding substitutes for hard to find replacement parts or equipment; to negotiations; to fixing that broken flushing mechanism in the janitors' toilet.

In the area of negotiations it is extremely important to conduct them in a professional manner and bring them to closure as soon as possible for, as most of you already know opportunities may not last long.

If you are negotiating housing leases for example, find out who your competition is. Are they artificially pushing up rent prices? If so, what do you do to bring them back down? A case in point is the U. S. Government's need for housing in foreign countries. The competition for units comes from companies in the private sector and international agencies such as the United Nations and the World Bank who are willing to spend humongous amounts of money on executive residences.

Some creative ways to get lower rents in this area include offering owners lump sum advance rent payments of up to 18 months or longer; offering to rent long term—five or six years with fixed escalating rent increases every year or two; putting a U.S. dollar clause in the contract so payments in the local currency maintain their value in case of a currency devaluation; and, if the company is providing its own furniture, furnishings and appliances possibly leaving expendable items such as drapes, or non-expendable equipment such as air conditioners, stoves or washers and dryers in place at the termination of the lease contract.

Another example I can give of creativity involved an American company in Bolivia that I was familiar with. The company had invested almost twelve million U.S. dollars in a mining venture that became unprofitable because of declining metal prices in the early 1980's. They decided to sell the mine to cut their losses and leave Bolivia. The asking price was in the neighborhood of six million U.S. dollars, in cash.

After months and months without any takers along come some creative young men trying to broker a 4.5 million U.S. dollar offer to be paid in existing mineral concentrates that the company they represented had located in Bolivia and at the port of Arica, Chile. The selling company said, "No deal, too risky we don't operate like that. It's cash or nothing." Three years later this mining venture was sold to a Bolivian mining company for less than one million U.S. dollars, but, paid for in cash!

The American company must have been delighted as they got what they wanted—cash. To me it did not sound like a good business transaction at all. One of the guys trying to broker the 4.5 million dollar sale; payable in mineral concentrates was one David Anthony Korponai. You win some and you lose some.

Along with the creative aspect of doing business or solving problems is the element of risk. (Identification and analysis of risk will be expanded on in a later discussion). The chance of risk in any number of areas normally rises in most overseas environments. This could even be true in High Human Development countries; particularly when a company is involved in a start-up operation and did not do due diligence in learning about the country that they are going into. The quote in my first book deserves repeating:

> *"To laugh is to risk appearing the fool.*
> *To weep is to risk appearing sentimental.*
> *To reach out for another is to risk involvement.*
> *To expose feelings is to risk exposing your true self.*
> *To place your ideas, your dreams before a crowd is to risk their loss.*
> *To love is to risk not being loved in return.*
> *To live is to risk dying.*
> *To hope is to risk despair.*
> *To try is to risk failure.*
> *But risks must be taken, because the greatest hazard in life is to risk nothing.*
> *The person who risks nothing does nothing, has nothing and is nothing. They*
> *May avoid suffering and sorrow but they cannot learn, feel, change, grow, love, live. Chained by their certitudes they are a slave, they have forfeited their freedom.*
> *Only a person who risks is free."*

I'll add to this another anonymous quote:

> *"The reason some men do not succeed is because their wishbone is where their backbone ought to be."*

Be as creative as you can in the overseas work environment. In being creative you may have to rock the boat; you may be viewed by some as a renegade or maverick. So what, you are a more effective manager, right?

A recent survey of American businessmen indicated that the most important quality that they look for in a new hire is not loyalty or dependability but—creativity.

Be Aware of the Significance of Being Creative, Thinking Outside of the Box and Even Rocking the Boat a Bit.

THREE-PEAT:

A More Effective Manager exercises excellent communication skills and gives instructions in a clear, concise and easily understood manner.

This may be more relevant to those of you working with blue collar workers. Drivers, warehousemen, maintenance workers or custodial staff fall into this area of consideration. You can also include any domestic help whom you may have hired to help at home. Likewise, repeating one's self to a local vendor in the marketplace is not uncommon at all.

Having to repeat one's self to elements of a foreign national work force may be frustrating. However, the purpose of this is to ensure that what you want done will be done correctly the first time. Work on developing language communication skills that will make your job more enjoyable.

The most common negative feedback that I have heard from foreign nationals is that Americans speak too fast and run words and sentences together. And, that we use too many *slang* expressions.

Slang expressions may not be understood or worst yet, literally interpreted. To tell a driver to "Go jump in the lake" and have him come back an hour later soaking wet would indicate a misunderstanding in what you really meant.

How do we break or modify these habits? One way is to be conscious that this is an area of concern to the foreign nationals that you will be supervising or working with and others outside of the work place as well. Remember to speak slower and in a clear voice. Give concise instructions. Integrate visual communicating skills such as pictures or, as they use in the Army, "arm and hand signals" in your talks. The bottom line is to get the message across. To get the person to understand just what it is that you are saying.

Remember also that communication is a two way street. You may not understand Farid Wadie Beshiet's response either. Do not be afraid or embarrassed to ask him to repeat himself. A good rule of thumb is to give instructions clear and concise; sometimes not only once but twice or thrice.

Along with this, be as specific as you can when giving instructions or doling out tasks. Think about the man who was given two wishes by the Good Fairy. He asked for the *best* wine and the *best* woman. The next moment he had the best wine on the table and Mother Teresa sitting beside him.

Be Aware of the Need to Hone Your Skills in Communication and Do Not Be Bashful of Three-peating.

GALABAYA TIME:
A More Effective Manager takes pride in his appearance and in the appearance of the staff that he manages.

People in some countries place a lot of emphasis on dress. Their attitude is: you dress like a tourist, you are a tourist; you dress like a professional, you are a professional; you dress like a bum, you are a bum.

Believe it or not, at some levels, including executive level dress will sometimes help establish the tone of a meeting. A case in point mentioned in my first book is worth repeating here. I set up a meeting in La Paz between three highly successful American miners and the Bolivian Minister of Mines. The Americans had made millions of dollars mining gold in Alaska. They came to Bolivia searching for alluvial deposits of gold in the hopes of starting a mining venture there. These guys came to the meetings wearing work boots, flannel shirts and jeans. They hadn't shaved in several days, and it showed. Why, because they had just returned from the field where they were looking at some investment properties that were owned by the GOB. And, quite frankly, they felt comfortable in their attire.

The minister took me aside at the conclusion of our ten minute meeting and said, "Señor David, these people are not really successful miners, no"? My reply was, "Si Señor Minister, they are worth millions of dollars." His comeback was—"Too bad, maybe I should have talked to them longer."

I am not saying that the brush off that these three men got from the Minister was the sole reason for them not returning to Bolivia but—you never know. My gut feeling was that the initial impression that they made on the Minister, even before they opened their mouths played a significant part in his evaluation of their presence and the tension that was in the air.

As Oliver Goldsmith said:

"An emperor in his night-cap would not meet with half respect of an emperor with a crown."

For you, dressing appropriately helps your image. It will help build confidence in your foreign national staff knowing that they are working with someone who not only cares about himself, but because of that will care about them as well.

This is not only true in the office environment. If you are in the area of supervising mostly tradesmen a clean and crisp uniform for the maintenance crew will add to the aura of professionalism. And the fact that you encouraged and supported their training and equipped them with the right tools to do their job didn't hurt either. What a good feeling you, the more effective manager will have as this well-trained crew, brimming with self-confidence and eager to serve the needs of the customers goes about their business. And don't forget about the company image that the janitorial and the warehouse staff and the company driver(s) should project.

Besides uniforms, and if needed give them a few hints related to personal hygiene and you're on your way to a more relaxing day at the office.

Having just mentioned the above, still have respect for the way that the foreign nationals on the staff dress. Remember that they may not have the income to spend on clothes like you do. Also, in some countries local dress standards may be carried into the work place. *Saris*, turbans, *galabayas* or *sarafans* may be the dress of the day.

Don't forget those "Casual Fridays" either. This may be something new or unfamiliar to some. You may not be able to convince that old geezer sitting in the corner; who has been brought up to wear a shirt and tie every day, sometimes a tattered and frayed shirt, but give it a shot. There is nothing wrong with coming into the office in clean jeans or slacks and a sport shirt.

Finally, try getting a $US50,000 bank loan dressed like Paris Hilton or Freddy the Freeloader. The old Gillette razor slogan was, "Look sharp, Feel Sharp, Be Sharp." Projecting an image of being successful will, in fact help you to become a more effective manager.

While this book focuses on performance in the work environment I would be remiss if I did not carry this particular discussion over and into the non-work environment. Take your professionalism with you. Forget the touristy, loud shirt and paisley pants look. This, plus the camera bag draped over your shoulder and the money belt bulging from your waist are dead giveaways that you are a foreigner in the host country.

I was in a restaurant in Kingston and in saunters this young white dude wearing plaid Bermuda shorts and a flowery short-sleeved shirt. He had tattoos up and down his arms and legs, a little Jamaican cap perched on this head and wearing sandals that displayed his lily white feet. Needless to say heads started turning his way. Try not to target yourself as a foreigner. Do your best to blend in with the locals.

Dress in a tasteful manner.

Be Aware of How Your Appearance Effects Not Only Employees in the Workplace But Your Customers As Well.

PATIENCE, PATIENCE AND MORE PATIENCE:

A More Effective Manager exercises patience from the time he gets up in the morning until the time he goes to bed at night.

Although this is mentioned and alluded to in other parts of this book, it is more than worthy of special reference and classification as a separate awareness element.

Patient is defined by Mr. Webster as; "1: bearing pains or trials calmly or without complaint. 2: manifesting forbearance under provocation or stress. 3: not hasty or impetuous. 4: steadfast despite opposition, difficulty, or adversity".

Accept beforehand that these definitions will indeed become an almost daily part of your management life in the overseas environment. If you do, you are well on your way to developing the habit of patience.

Kid yourself not—Your patience will be tried, tested and tried again on an almost daily basis. This including most weekends and holidays.

It took me almost seven months to negotiate a one million U.S. dollar mining contract in Bolivia. It required many trips by four wheel drive vehicle, boat, and foot to the mining concession itself, countless meetings with the directorate of the cooperative and our local attorney, and many fax's and telephone calls to the home office in the United States. The contract was finally agreed upon by both parties and the signing date set for 16 April. On 14 April I received a telephone call from the president of the American company that the deal was off.

The point of this example—Your patience will not only be tried within the overseas work environment, but it may also be tried by your home office as well. Why? I have found that many organizations and companies tend to micro-manage the overseas operation from the home office. I am not saying being over-sighted from the home office, I am saying being *micro-managed* by the home office. The fear of losing control may contribute to this attitude. In the private sector, the fear of nationalization of the company by the host country government may be a consideration. Whatever the reason, be prepared for this.

The president of S.J. Groves & Sons probably summed it up for the private sector when he asked, "Why should I go 3,000 miles to Bolivia to risk losing money when I may run the same risk by bidding a job in California—and, with fewer headaches"! While S.J. Groves & Sons may have lost money on the road project in Bolivia (their first project in South America), they positioned themselves for future projects by having equipment in country, trained local national staff and a highly motivated and knowledgeable ex-patriot staff. So what did they do when the project was completed? You guessed it. They pulled up stakes and left. No guts, no glory. No patience, no profit.

Be Aware of the Demand to Exercise a High Degree of Patience While Working in a Foreign Country.

A POSITIVE ATTITUDE:

A More Effective Manager never underestimates the power of positive thinking.

This is even more important in an overseas environment than it is in the home country environment.

Why? Good question. Let me try to answer it by starting with a positive quote credited to Winston Churchill;

> *"A pessimist sees the difficulty in every opportunity; an optimist sees the opportunity in every difficulty."*

There are more variables in an overseas environment; some of which are not only beyond your control, but light-years away from your control. These can have a negative impact on what you do or how you feel. And, many times these variables pop up with little or no warning. Quite simply put, you will find more things to bitch about in a foreign environment. Like what? How about electrical power failures, waiting two hours for the photocopier repairman to show up on Wednesday (he never showed up on Monday) and not being able to get an outside phone line to call your home office.

Don't fret. I believe that while things mentioned in the above paragraph are inevitable, all is not lost. Why? Because you will find it challenging and exciting to live and work in an environment that you are not familiar with. You are a more effective manager; you thrive on challenges, right?

Realize that you are not the first person to be put in some of the situations that you will be in, nor will you be the last. I knew a couple, in their mid to late fifty's from Wharton, Texas who had never been east of the Mississippi River let alone overseas. It was one big adjustment for them to make coming to Cairo, Egypt from Wharton. Yet, I do not believe that I have ever met a couple with a more positive attitude in the overseas environment. Paul and Beverly, we love ya!

Your positive attitude will help you to focus on other awareness elements in the work environment such as time management and patience. This will facilitate your managing in a more efficient and more effective manner. Believe me, your positive attitude will help you through many a trying day. To be a more effective manager you must have a positive attitude.

There was an article in the *Financial Times* several years ago that dealt with work. The three reasons identified as causing one to be miserable at work were: the work itself, the people and the general environment. What can you influence with a positive attitude? Almost certainly not the work itself; if you dislike the work, you probably need to find another career.

General environment is broad but in this discussion let's narrow it down to the physical aspects only; crowded workspaces, no eating facility in the plant or other eateries nearby, unclean toilet facilities, etcetera. Maybe your positive attitude towards change can encourage others to put on their creative thinking caps and come up with alternative solutions to some of the missing amenities.

Related to crowded work space now is the common use of cubicles. Those of you thrust into this environment for the first time and no longer in a private office may have to modify the way that you conduct some of your business. Interviews for example or discussing personal or sensitive information may have to be tempered. You better develop a positive attitude knowing that your coworkers on half the floor can hear you when you blow your nose or pass gas.

What your attitude can have the most significant impact on, in my opinion is on the other people in the workplace. Changing a negative mind-set of others to a positive one can have an impact on such things as improving quality of work, reducing tardiness and apathy, meeting deadlines and most important, fostering teamwork and reducing employee stress. And, showing a fierce sense of optimism will instill confidence and trust in your subordinates.

Besides, your positive attitude may bring a little humor into someone's life. In 2011 I bought a used, 1996 Nissan Sunny in Kingston. My friend, in a somewhat sarcastic way asked me that since the car was so old if I knew where to buy spare parts. I told him "No" I didn't because I would not have to buy any used parts! He scratched his head and laughed and walked away with a smile on his face and leaving the comment to me of; "Yea mon, right." Time will tell.

If you think times are tough; focus on the fact that tough times never last, tough people do. This comes about more easily to folks with a positive attitude. And remember that the making of a living is not the same as the making of a life.

Your positive attitude will roll over into your personal life as well. It may even begin there. The affect that it will have on your family and friends will be rewarding and heartfelt.

Be Aware of the Good a Positive Attitude Brings to the Workplace.

INGREDIENTS IN THE WORK ENVIRONMENT:

A More Effective Manager discovers and identifies various ingredients in the host country work environment.

Let me try to explain this like so. Some of the "ingredients" I will mention are related to interpersonal relationships; management/ organization; problem solving skills of the indigenous employee; investment in people; and, technology. There may be more where you are. If so, add them to your list.

In late 1969 I was sitting with a Bolivian friend of mine and we were discussing the growth ingredients needed in Low Human Development (LHD) countries (In 1969 I would have placed Bolivia in this category). I said, "Juan, LHD countries need three things for growth: foreign capital investment; technology; and strong management". Juan's reply was; "We also need immigration." He was absolutely correct so I added this to my list of growth ingredients. I might add at this time that he was referring to a controlled, legal immigration.

In the area of management/organization—are your employees friendly towards one another? Do they work together as a team? Do they share ideas and suggestions with one another? Is there synergism in the work place? These need to be developed if they are missing.

Of importance also is the organization of the unit that you are managing. Is it top heavy? Maybe there are too many chiefs and not enough Indians? In countries where labor is "cheap", be on the lookout for real productivity and the quality that you get from cheap labor. Maybe you will need two secretaries to do what you thought one could do. Will the extra fifty cents a day be the incentive to increase productivity by forty percent? It could be.

Problem Solving Skills—Become aware of the problem solving skills of employees in the work force that you manage. If this ingredient is lacking, you will probably find yourself spending more time supervising your supervisors than you expected.

Technology—Are you keeping abreast with developments or becoming complacent because it is too much work to train local staff on new equipment? Does your computer hardware or software need updating?

Investment in people—Will you have to fight with your home office to get them to reinvest more of their profits into salaries or training of employees or improving working conditions?

A more effective manager will develop a feeling for the ingredients in the work place that will allow her to manage better, smarter and more effectively.

Be Aware of the Ingredients in the Work Environment.

CHANGING THE PARADIGM:

A More Effective Manager meets the challenge of changing paradigms head on.

Mr. Webster defines paradigm as; "1: Example, Pattern, esp.: an outstanding clear or typical example or archetype".

Let's jump to Washington, D.C. for a few moments to better understand this. The buzz words/phrases in Washington management circles are still along the lines of: Look for ways to change existing paradigms; let's re-invent government and re-engineer; we have to do more with less. But, you really don't hear very much about maintaining or improving quality of services or whatever or about Total Quality Management—TQM.

As the United States moved from a manufacturing base to a service performance base, the importance of identifying customers and their needs seemed to have been reignited and rejuvenated. However, the idea of customer service is not new. Nor has the concept of providing a quality product to users changed.

Changing paradigms revolves around asking the question "Why"? Why are we doing it this way? Why are we designing this auto along these lines? Why do our customers like this? "Why"? "Why"? "Why"?

The answer to the "Why" question should lead to the most efficient utilization of all available resources, including manpower and capital. It can also lead to paradigm shifts.

Reinventing (Changing?) government is not a new concept but still seems a bit baffling to some. It is important to understand the difference between the government and the state; governments may come and go, but, the state remains. Reinventing government is changing the way that any government administration operates. For example—Streamlining procedures or changing legislature as to where tax dollars are spent.

Back to TQM—Total Quality Management may be a change to an existing paradigm. It advocates that everyone is your customer; from your client to your secretary. Everyone, at all levels plays a role in the process. Everyone becomes a shareholder. OK, now let's see how this fits into the management scheme overseas.

First, you have to buy into three realities: 1. Change takes time; 2. Change will meet resistance; and, 3. Change involves taking a risk. If you find this true in the home country environment, and I believe that you will, then it is even truer in a foreign country, in particular those countries that are on the lower part of the upward slope of the development curve.

Why will a change that you want to make meet resistance? For one reason, the change is coming from a foreigner, a stranger; someone who is not familiar with the customs and traditions of the host country (But, you've overcome this right?). For another, the attitude might be: It's been done this way since Christ was a corporal—Why change it now? Yet another, host country bureaucracy may impede the implementation of any proposed changes.

Change takes time. Growing pains are inevitable. You will undoubtedly hear comments along the lines of, "Go ahead, try it, it will take forever to get it changed." "Hell will freeze over before anyone sees this change."

Changing the paradigm may also mean taking a risk. The quote regarding risk taking mentioned earlier is apropos here as well. And if you are a real risk taker follow the advice I heard from a fast tracking female executive not too long ago. When asked about her strategy about making decisions about program implementation before bureaucrats sitting 3,000 miles away gave her the go ahead—"I don't ask for permission but I may later ask for forgiveness."

Implementing change or changing paradigms in the work environment is not easy. It is difficult in the home country and it is even more difficult in the host country. If you believe that a change is needed, go for it. The more effective manager must have the patience and perseverance to see it through. He must also have the understanding that he may not see the results of his efforts and may have to leave the implementation of any proposed change to his replacement or, to his replacement's replacement or to his replacement's, replacement's replacement—Get the picture?

Be Aware of the Factors Involved in Trying to Change the Paradigm When Working in Some Foreign Countries.

PRIOR PLANNING:

A More Effective Manager puts a maximum effort into the prior planning of work or events and anticipating unforeseen problems.

If the importance of prior planning is stressed by your organization at home, it should be stressed twice or three times as much in the overseas work environment.

Why?—Usually because there are more areas where things can go wrong: whatever it is that you do, don't become stubborn or take a myopic point of view and not admit to this. Delays in getting things through customs for instance and delays in receiving items sent through international mail may be common in some countries. Misunderstanding because of language, even between professionals, is still another area to be wary of. How about the movement of supplies, equipment or goods by poor host country transportation systems including rail and roads?

The Six P's discussed in my first book: Prior Planning Prevents Piss Poor Performance should be chiseled into the mind of every more effective manager working in an overseas environment. To do this you have to gather as much information as you can about whatever it is that you are planning.

Furthermore, and mark my words no matter how much you've planned something it will still not go exactly as you planned it! Murphy's Law, if something can go wrong, it will go wrong is the gospel truth. A motto—"Prepare for the worst, hope for the best," comes to mind.

And don't forget to plan for those visits from people from the home office. If you're lucky enough to land a job in some exotic place like Fiji, the Bahamas or Monaco or a multinational place like Montevideo, Uruguay or Zurich, Switzerland you can expect more frequent visits.

Those of you in one of your government's agencies overseas may want to learn a bit from a recent article concerning visits to Pakistan by officials from Washington and how distracting that they were to the diplomatic mission there. How's this:

> "In 2009, the embassy hosted almost 700 such travelers, including members of Congress, high-ranking administration officials and staffers who traveled to Pakistan to meet with top U.S. diplomats and Pakistani leaders. Embassy officials conducted at least 100 preparatory meetings before the visits and tied up 300 embassy-owned vehicles during a total of 175 days in Pakistan."

Obviously some of these were necessary. But how many were self-serving visits to reach out to voters, to bolster one's reputation within an Agency or to move up the career ladder.

For those of you involved in vehicle or equipment procurement or maintenance prior planning is an area of special interest. Maybe you can't get a Ford serviced in some places in Zimbabwe. If not, then how about considering a right hand four-wheel drive, Toyota with a high wheel base?

When S.J. Groves & Sons was selected for the road construction job in Bolivia they brought into that country nearly eight million U.S. dollars' worth of new equipment. Most of the heavy equipment was Caterpillar, the compressors and drills were Joy and the light vehicles were Ford. They also brought in nearly one and one-half million U.S. dollars' worth of spare parts and even more important, eight American mechanics. Good planning right?

Prior planning involves among other things getting all the facts and thinking things through. Let me end this discussion on the light side with a piece recently floating around the internet:

> *"Arcelor-Mittal Steel, feeling it as time for a shakeup hired a new CEO. The new boss was determined to rid the company of all slackers.*
>
> *On a tour of the facilities, the CEO noticed a guy leaning against a wall in one of the workshops. The room was full of workers and he wanted to let them know that he meant business. He asked the guy, 'How much money do you make a week.'*

A little surprised, the young man looked at him and said, 'I make $400 a week. Why?'

The CEO said, 'Wait right here.' He walked back to his office, came back 2 minutes later and handed the guy $1,600 in cash and said, 'Here's four weeks' pay. Now GET OUT and don't come back.'

Feeling pretty good about himself, the CEO waited till the guy left and then looked around the workshop and asked, 'Does anyone want to tell me what the goof-ball did here?'

From across the room a voice said, 'He's the pizza delivery guy from Dominos.''

Be Aware of the Importance of Gathering Information, Prior Planning and Anticipation.

Special Interest Areas

PUBLIC RELATIONS:
A More Effective Manager is a Public Relations person.

This may involve selling yourself as well as the company or organization. The image that you project of yourself, as a foreigner in the host country and the image that you project as a manager becomes the image of your organization or company—the "corporate" image." Need I say more?

Public relations may involve imaging or branding. I remember talking to a past Administrator of USAID. He asked me what I thought would make a positive impact on the organization. I suggested he hire a Public Relations company to tell the American people that foreign aid is a necessary part of the U.S. Government's overall strategy to make the world a better place to live in.

The image that the USG was throwing away money through USAID type assistance programs was simply not true. It was the Development "D" in the three "D" concept of Defense, Diplomacy and Development as a foreign affairs policy.

A few years after my conversation with the Administrator, USAID went through a branding exercise that included a new logo and motto (From the American People). Whether or not my comment to him had any impact on this decision or not is really not important to me. What was important was that I expressed my opinion, and maybe even rocked the boat a bit by suggesting the commercialization of USAID and that this Administrator at least listened to what I had to say.

Good PR will also help rid the company of that "Ugly American" baggage that it may still carry because your predecessor was not keenly aware of the importance of projecting a positive company image; one of making a *fair* profit or being a *fair* employer.

Getting back to you, I have found that in many countries titles and degrees are very important. Don't feel ashamed to acknowledge your accomplishments or completion of your university degree(s) or post graduate degree(s) or specialty training. For whatever reason, it adds to your credibility in whatever area that you are working in.

Be sure to put any accreditations on your business cards. Everyone may not know what RN, BS, CNOR (E), CRNFA (E) or CPSN (E) stand for but, you earned them.

Be Aware of Paying Attention to the Role of Public Relations in Whatever You Do.

NEGOTIATIONS:
A More Effective Manager knows when to exercise the art of negotiation.

Regardless of your position, your negotiating skills will undoubtedly come into play more often than you might think.

The reasons for a need to negotiate are damn near ad nauseam, especially in Low Human Development countries. They range from various contracting matters such as negotiating personal or non-personal service contracts, leasing of real estate property such as houses, apartments or office space and local purchases of supplies, materials or equipment.

And don't forget the possibility of labor negotiations. I will once again steal something from my first book. When I was with the S.J. Groves & Sons company in Bolivia we were having some problems with the *sindicato* or labor union. I had to negotiate various pay and allowance matters with a judge from the Minister of Labor. She was so damn tough and competent that after my second visit I recommended to my boss that we hire her to represent the company in all labor matters. After negotiating with my boss, my recommendation was accepted. For a relatively small investment, the company got a labor specialist who knew the local laws inside and out, plus knew the local court system. My negotiation with my boss gave me more peace of mind. Basically, we hired her away from the GOB.

Again with SJ Groves & Sons—Another area of negotiation that I found somewhat difficult to accept was the need to negotiate with the home office for changes in the overseas operation. This is not only often the case in the private sector but with home country governmental agencies as well. As I have already mentioned, for whatever reason, I have found that many companies or organizations tend to micro manage the overseas operation. They are reluctant to decentralize not only functions and responsibilities, but authority as well to the executive or manager of the foreign operation. The need to *control* and the feel of *power* oftentimes clouds good judgment.

Granted, there are certain areas that are best left in the hands of the home office. But unfortunately you still might find that cutting through the host country red tape is simpler than cutting through your own company's or organizations' bureaucratic red tape.

Be Aware of the Necessity to Hone Negotiating Skills.

TRAVELIN' ON:
A More Effective Manager understands the effect that travel can have on employee morale and well-being.

No matter where you are you will hear stories about travel. They will be related to a host of things from cost, ticketing, travel and airport waiting time, seating, food, other passengers, etcetera, etcetera, and etcetera. Some of the stories I heard:

Travel on a Middle Eastern airline that does not allow passengers to bring animals on board with them. The exception; seeing-eye dogs and falcons!

A seventeen-hour train ride, in Tajikistan by a solo, non-Tajik speaking passenger in July, on the milk run that stops every half hour or so, seated in economy class in a car shared by dozens and dozens or foul-smelling locals and farm animals. An upgraded ticket could have been purchased for a seat in a compartment shared by only three others for ten dollars more.

While the military men did not have a choice in this next incident, picture this; young men on a seven day cruise across the blue Atlantic on a military transport from the Brooklyn Army Terminal in New York to Bremerhaven, Germany. Most of the time was spent in a cramped troop compartment, below water line, sleeping on hammock-type bunks stacked four high—some with mid-western kids who had never been on a boat before. These kids were turning green and spending most of the day up-chucking their breakfast of powdered eggs and Sh!t-On-a-Shingle (SOS).

But there are some positive stories also. A lot of the long train runs in Eastern Europe and Russia leave in the early evening and arrive at their final destination early morning. If you can grab some shut eye on the train you have a very cost effective means to see the country. One schedule looked something like this:

6:40 p.m. Monday	depart Kiev, Ukraine
8:30 a.m. Tuesday	arrive Moscow, Russia
11:40 p.m. Tuesday	depart Moscow
8:00 a.m. Wednesday	arrive Saint Petersburg, Russia
11:40 p.m. Wednesday	depart Saint Petersburg
8:00 a.m. Thursday	arrive Moscow
8:20 p.m. Thursday	depart Moscow
10:30 a.m. Friday	arrive Kiev

No hotel costs and two full days to enjoy Moscow and one full day to enjoy Saint Petersburg.

Be Aware of Finding Yourself a Very Good Travel Agent.

HOST COUNTRY CURRENCY (MONEY MATTERS):

A More Effective Manager pays close attention to foreign currency policy in the host country and the effect that it can have on the company's operation or on his personal way of life.

There are a host of areas to take into consideration in this element. These include: convertibility of host country currency into U.S. dollars or home country currency; rates of exchange between currencies; availability of a foreign currency for export of profits; use of Letters of Credit; host country inflation and currency devaluations; and, payments in host country currency.

Rather than discuss in detail any of the above, let me give you several examples of what can happen in the real world.

The contract that S.J. Groves & Sons had with the Government of Bolivia (GOB) to build the road in Bolivia called for payments of monthly completed works. Twenty-five percent of the payment was to be made in local currency (Pesos Bolivianos) and seventy-five percent of the payment was to be in U.S. dollars. The U.S. dollar payment was made by the International Development Bank (IDB). The IDB would not release payments until the GOB had made the peso portion of the payment.

You got it! Late payments by the GOB delayed payments by the IDB. Since the peso payments were to be used for local purchases and expenditures, and they were not forthcoming on time, S.J. Groves had to wire transfer U.S. dollars into their account in Bolivia and convert them into pesos in order to keep the project going. Guess who paid for the wire transfer and other related costs?

Mining in Chile—The mining law is very clear. In the mid-1980s the Government of Chile (GOC) received five percent of production. Let's take gold. The GOC could have asked for this five percent in one of three ways: 1. in production. You mine one hundred ounces of gold in any given month, the GOC receives five ounces; 2. in U.S. dollars. The GOC receives the equivalent in U.S. dollars of the value of five ounces of gold on the day of payment to them; 3. in Chilean Pesos. The GOC receives the equivalent in Chilean Pesos of the value of five ounces of gold on the day of payment to them. Controls related to quantities were established and based on material assays of either raw ore or slurry gold content.

Devaluation—Bolivia—A classic example. From early February to late November 1982 the Peso Boliviano devalued against the U.S. dollar (USD) eleven times. It went from 24.51 Bolivianos to 1.00 USD to 500.00 Bolivianos to 1.00 USD. This was followed by a "floating" rate of exchange for several months. This was easy. When the "official" rate was in the neighborhood of 1,076 Bolivianos to 1.00 USD and the "black market" rate was in the neighborhood of 3,500 Bolivianos it really got to be fun! How does this affect your accounting methods with your home office as you try to balance general ledger accounts?

You may hear foreigners refer to local currency in some countries as "funny money" or "Monopoly money." This stems from the fact that in some countries paper money is printed in various colors depending on the value of the bill. And it may have some very unusual printed matter   on it other than the value denomination.

As an individual, you may want to look closely into how to exchange currency on the local market. In addition to banks, many countries have exchange houses that offer to exchange money at government controlled/regulated exchange rates. There may also be an unsanctioned, underground black market where one can exchange currency on the street corner of from the car window. In all cases, ask what the rate of exchange is that you are getting and count and recount the money you receive.

Be Aware of Host Country Fiscal Policies.

RISK IDENTIFICATION AND ANALYSIS:
A More Effective Manager puts forth maximum effort in identifying and assessing risks.

This is not only true on the home-front but probably more so in an overseas environment. It is true whether you are starting up, maintaining, expanding or closing an operation in a foreign country.

In the early 1980s I researched and wrote my thesis, ***The Identification and Analysis of Business Risks in an Overseas Environment: the Bolivian Experience.*** As a starting point, and based on my experiences in Bolivia I identified thirty-three (33) risks which I categorized into four major areas: Financial; Political; Social; and, Internal. Through my literary research I identified fifteen (15) more risks that I placed within the four categories mentioned above. As a result of my interviews with twenty-five successful Bolivian and twenty-five successful foreign business people working in Bolivia, a total of twenty-six (26) more surfaced which I again categorized and added to the four major areas. In summary, using these three information sources, seventy-four (74) potential risks were identified (See Appendix C).

Some of you may be wondering why I did not ask the end users or "customers" of the businesspeople I interviewed for their input. Good point. I made a decision as to the methodology to use to arrive at conclusions. I did not feel at that time, and in retrospective I do not feel at this time, that this group would have provided input that would have significantly changed any of my findings, since they were obtained after an extensive literary review and interview of the fifty, proven successful business people. These people had their finger on the daily pulse of the business community and knew the general business climate in county.

Are there more than these seventy-four risks to consider? The answer is—Probably so. Also, some of you may feel that some of the risks identified are not applicable to the country that you will be working in or to the type of business that you are involved in. While some of the risks that I identified may have been more Bolivia specific, I found that the majority were in fact, applicable in every other country that I have worked in.

There is certainly some connectivity between prior planning and risk taking. Remember the Six-Ps of planning; Prior Planning Prevents Piss Poor Performance. Done well, risk is reduced; done poorly and the chance of risk in enhanced. However, identifying risk is one thing—not being afraid to take it is another.

Be Aware of the Need of Risk Identification and Analysis.

EXPEDITING FEES:
A More Effective Manager is thoughtful when it comes to paying expediting fees.

These are those fees related to getting things processed through customs or through one of the host country ministries; those fees associated with keeping things moving through various processes such as delivery of supplies or foodstuffs; those fees that may help to grease the skids for negotiating your next contract with whomever; etcetera.

More bluntly, this normally refers to host country graft and corruption in the form of payoffs to employees, usually those in the public sector. This could be an extremely sensitive issue to the foreign manager who may even be subject to home country laws. In the United

States for example, the Foreign Corrupt Practices Act of 1977, as amended, 15 U.S.C. prevails and addresses issues along these lines. This was enacted for the purpose of making it unlawful for certain classes of persons or entities to make payments to foreign government officials to assist in obtaining business.

How about considering some real examples and looking at them from the common sense, practical point of view. During the time that S.J. Groves & Sons was in Bolivia it normally took anywhere from five to ten work days to process the paperwork to clear something through customs and receive the item(s). Custom's clearance was done by a registered Bolivian customer's broker who was engaged to provide this service. Normally never less than five days, but at times more than ten days, a lot longer than ten days I might add. But, by paying *expediting* fees to customs' officials the broker could get something out in twenty-four hours. What do you do when you have a D9 tractor sitting in the maintenance shop because the $13.00 gasket needed to get it up and running again is sitting on someone's desk in the customs' office?

One way to get around the system without having to worry about expediting fees was to have a passenger on the flight from Miami to La Paz hand-carry small items in their luggage. That's right, it was less expensive to pay a passenger twenty-five or thirty US dollars to hand carry small items.

How about those holiday gifts to officials who play a role in approving documents related to customs, getting the company vehicles registered or the approval to export something? Will a bottle of Scotch do it? How about a case? Is this a thank you for helping to expedite or payola?

At Thanksgiving/Christmas time, while working for S.J. Groves & Sons we shipped frozen turkeys from Miami to La Paz for our thirty American, ex-pat employees. Three of these frozen birds fit into one, Styrofoam lined foot locker. Thirty ex-pats times eleven foot lockers equaled thirty-three birds. These were cleared through customs in a matter of minutes, and you got it, three Bolivian families were also happier and better fed for the holidays.

You may have to wrestle with the idea that the payment of expediting fees may be the normal way of doing business in the host country. Other companies from other countries do it, right? No matter what your role is in a situation that may involve the concept of expediting fees, abide by home country and host country laws and regulations and let your conscience be your guide.

Let me ramble on a bit here and at the risk of sounding a bit cynical, I have not worked in any country that has not been tainted with accusation of and incidents of graft—including the United States.

When I was in Oklahoma working on my thesis there was a big to-do about county assessors undervaluing properties in exchange of getting their driveway paved, a swimming pool dug out, landscaping done on their property, etcetera. If I remember correctly it was costing the state of Oklahoma 20 million US dollars of lost revenue per annum. And this was Oklahoma—what goes on in Illinois, New York, California or other more populated and politically heavy-weight states.

But here's the big difference when rule of law prevails in any country. The assessors who committed these dastardly deeds in Oklahoma where brought to trial and paid the price by losing their jobs or being fined and/or incarcerated. This may not be the case in some other countries.

Be Aware of Payment of Expediting Fees That May be Perceived as Bribes.

YOUR DYNAMIC DUO:
  A More Effective Manager will quickly realize the importance of her attorney and banker.

Regardless of how you are organized, include these two people on your team. You have to find individuals whom you have trust and confidence in and with whom you can communicate with. Sounds pretty basic doesn't it? But they may not be an easy find, especially if the language barrier cannot be bridged.

During the first eighteen months that S.J. Groves & Sons was in Bolivia they changed their attorney four times before settling for a Bolivian, Harvard educated corporate attorney. The fact that he was associated with a well-established, family firm and had good local and international business and Government of Bolivia connections didn't hurt either. This attorney probably saved the company hundreds of thousands of dollars through his work with officials in the GOB and his interpretation of not only the contractual agreement but of GOB policy and regulation as well.

Depending on your business you may opt to consider attorneys who specialize in certain fields. It is imperative to find an attorney knowledgeable of local labor laws. Bolivia is heavily into mining and therefore there are a number of excellent attorneys who specialize in this field. In Kazakhstan, look for someone with a thorough knowledge of the petroleum sector.

Your banker is another person with whom you must develop a special relationship with. Rely on her to keep the pulse on currency exchange rates and host government financial policy. In most cases these are extremely complicated and in some Low and Medium Human Development countries where hyper-inflation may run rampant, they are very difficult to keep track of.

The timing of importing or exporting capital may have a significant impact on you profit and loss statement at the end of the quarter. For those of you in a business that is trying to make a profit, you might want to keep recalling what Charles Frederick Abbott had to say about that:

> *"Business without profit is not business any more than a pickle is candy."*

Banking instruments such as letters of credit and wire transfers may be vital to keep your operation competitive or operative in a host country.

While I can cite countless more examples as to why these two people should become key players on your team, let's put this one to rest. Develop your own reality test as to what your real needs are in these areas and assess and continue to reassess these needs. And don't forget that this relationship must, not should but must be based on *trust*.

Be Aware of the Importance of Your Dynamic Duo—Your Attorney and Banker.

POLITICS AND POLICY:
A More Effective Manager keeps tabs on host country politics and policy, and possible host country government shifts in either.

Host country politics can have a profound effect on how a company does business in that country. This is especially true when a government changes and along with it, different policies are enacted or existing policies are interpreted differently. The case in point here is the trend now in some countries to elect "populist" candidates. Also, shifts to the right or left seem to be the norm in a few countries. While it is incumbent upon the new manager to learn about this subject this also emphasizes the need to engage an exceptionally good attorney and banker.

On the policy front let me give you several examples of what I mean.

Ownership—Some countries require a certain percentage of ownership of a foreign company by host country participants—some as high as fifty-one per cent. Is your company prepared to get involved in this kind of a joint venture?

Operations—In the mining sector in Bolivia, it is prohibited for a foreign company to work in a ten kilometer area contiguous to a neighboring country. While there may be excellent opportunities to mine ten kilometers from the Chilean, Peruvian, Brazilian, Paraguayan, or Argentine border a foreign mining company cannot. Solution, form a joint venture with a Bolivian company. And, give up fifty-one percent control of the operation, right?

Importation—There may be some restrictions as to the quantity and type of materials that you may be allowed to import into a foreign country. You may be forced to use some local materials even though they may be of inferior quality. Host country policy along these lines may be to ensure filling internal consumption need and to protect local markets. In Jamaica you cannot import a car that is more than three years old or an SUV that is more than four years old.

Financial—What is the host country government doing to keep inflation under control? What is their policy concerning currency devaluation? How about export of capital gains?

In my opinion one of the biggest concerns for companies working in Low Human Development or politically unstable countries is the fear of nationalization or just being kicked out of the country. Nationalization of a company most often entails some sort of compensation to the company by the host country government. While loss of assets is inevitable, some return on a company's investment may be forthcoming. Getting booted out of a country may mean loss of assets with no hope of any restitution.

Prior knowledge of a country's political history and climate may in fact influence a company's decision not to engage in operations at all. While one could devote much more time discussing politics and its' impact on business or other activities, keep it simple. If your company is already established in country, you as a new manager should focus and do your best to develop an understanding of the major political power bases and their attitudes towards foreign businesses, foreign volunteer or humanitarian organizations or foreign governments. And, don't forget to keep your home office informed of any turn in events in this area.

Host country policy and politics go together. As a more effective manager, keep tuned to these.

Be Aware of Host Country Politics and Policy.

CHAPTER V

⟫•◆•⟪

CLOSING

THAT'S IT LADIES and gentlemen. Managing people while you are employed or serving overseas and adapting in a foreign country is as challenging as it is rewarding. Seeing results of your efforts in a place far from home is extremely gratifying.

As a foreigner working in this environment you can bring excitement, enthusiasm and new ideas into the work place. You also can cause a bit of apprehension to the players already on board. But, by being aware of the awareness elements discussed you can minimize this apprehension to a manageable degree from the start.

Showing folks in the work environment an inquisitiveness about them, their work and their country, at the beginning will help foster a working relationship that will make your managing less difficult. Show them your adaptability and willingness to learn *from* them and you will be seen as a more effective manager in the eyes of not only those you manage but hopefully in the eyes of your peers and supervisors as well.

AUTHOR'S AFTERWORD

HAVING HAD THE opportunity to live and work overseas as long as I have, and although sounding a bit like an oxymoron when compared to some other parts of this book I would like to mention, in my opinion the importance of keeping contact with family and friends. For most people who do not travel widely, this is most often a routine that goes without saying. For those folks in a more transient environment that may include separations, or in more isolated cases a lengthy disconnect with their own roots it may be a bittersweet lifestyle.

Maintaining some type of connectivity with family and friends will make it less difficult for you to not only return to your grassroots but to your country as well, even as an infrequent visitor. Staying in contact with people has been made easier through emails, face-book, Skype or whatever. But don't forget the occasional phone call to or a visit with an old Army buddy or a trip to attend a wedding, birthday, funeral or class reunion. The little ditty going around the internet mentioned that:

> *"Friendship is like a book. It takes a few seconds to burn, but it may take years to write."*

There are other reasons to try to go his route. Some of these persons may be future references or resources. Maintaining friendships is a no-brainer. Developing future friendships or companionships is another.

I know of a well-traveled retired U.S. Government employee who went back to a small town in Texas to live after having spent many years living and working abroad. Her main concern was to be able to find enough *locals* to talk to. The breadth and scope of local news and events was a lot narrow than what she was accustomed to after all of her years in the Foreign Service. Her connectivity with a longtime friend whom she shared this concern with about 3 or 4 months before her retirement made for a much smoother adjustment for her.

And, it's *fun* to maintain, renew or to even make new friends from the old gang. Some who may be even more interesting than you, the wayward overseas traveler are. If that happens, think of it as a new adventure. While the following may appear to be a bit corny, it is true none-the-less. At my 50th high school reunion I happened to meet someone who's CV read along the following lines:

Registered nurse
Pilot
Skydiver
Architect/Interior decorator/Landscaper
Fashion/Jewelry designer
Writer/Editor
Musician
Motivational Speaker
Gourmet Cook
Antique collector
Sportswoman
Woodcarver/Leatherworker/Caner
Linguist
Political activist
Innovator
Light auto mechanic
Stockbroker
County official
Photographer
Animal Trainer

Throw in mother and grandmother and worldwide traveler and about the only thing that this young lady probably had not gotten into was welding, with either hand as she is also ambidextrous.

Concluding with something that I had mentioned previously; *working in an overseas environment is not for everyone.* If you decide to go down this road, be aware of the pitfalls that may lie ahead, keep a positive attitude and be ready for one heck of a ride and *daring* adventure.

AUTHOR'S BIOGRAPHY

MR. KORPONAI HAS been with the United States Agency for International Development since January 1991. He served in Bolivia as the Supervisory General Service's Officer and Deputy Executive Officer, in Egypt as the Supervisory General Service's Officer, in Kazakhstan as the Executive Officer, in the Ukraine as the Deputy Executive Officer, in Montenegro as the Executive Officer and at this writing in Jamaica as the Executive Officer.

These management and logistical support activities provided services to over hundreds of American employees and their families and Foreign Service National employees. He also played key roles in developing Mission procurement plans and operating expense budgets; developing, drafting and implementing internal Mission management systems and policies; conducting management assessments; contract negotiations; developing and writing Statements of Work; and, coordinating security issues with USAID and American embassy personnel.

Prior to working with USAID, he worked for two large American companies in Bolivia. He was the administrative/financial manager for a 68 million U.S. dollar road construction project being built between La Paz and Cotapata Bolivia by the S.J. Groves & Sons Company, Minneapolis, Minnesota.

Following S.J. Groves & Sons he was the South American representative for the R. A. Hanson Company, Spokane, Washington. This company was involved in mining activities and the manufacture of mining and specialty equipment. In addition to his work in Bolivia he traveled to Chile, Ecuador and Brazil and assessed gold mining possibilities. In Chile he also established a network that led to the sale of equipment to GOC and private sector entities.

Mr. Korponai was honorably discharged from the United States Army in 1978 at the rank of Captain. His overseas tours included Germany, Vietnam (two tours) and Bolivia. He was retired from the United States Army Reserves at the rank of Major.

He graduated from the University of Connecticut in 1964 with a B.S. in Physical Education and earned a Master's degree in Business Management from LaSalle University in 1994.

Mr. Korponai published his first book, **Solving Management's Puzzle—The Art of Managing People** in 2009 with Trafford Publishing. He also had two articles published in *THE VANGUARD*, a USAID publication for Foreign Service Officers around the world. His first, "*The 'Gobbleizaiton' of USAID*" was published in December 2007, Volume 1, Issue 7 and the second, "*Is the System Broken?*" in 2008, Volume 2, Issue 3. His thesis, *Identification and Analysis of Business Risks in an Overseas Environment: The Bolivian Experience* was completed in 1993 and is registered in the U.S. Copyright Office, TXU000623849/1994-02-04.

He is married and has three grown children and five grand-children.

APPENDIX A

---◆◆◆---

Brief of Awareness Elements Discussed in the Author's First Book, *Solving Management's Puzzle—the Art of Managing People*

MOST, IF NOT all of the 56 awareness elements mentioned in my first book, ***Solving Management's Puzzle—The Art of Managing People*** are applicable to working in an overseas environment. To further whet the readers appetite for this, I will briefly hi-light some of the main points that were made.

Don't panic! You do not have to use or incorporate every awareness element into a particular managing or supervising situation. Use these as points of reference in your everyday managing activities.

1. *Your Most Precious Resource; People*

   - An employer makes an investment in each of his employees
   - Retention of competent employees is paramount to the success of an organization
   - Become a "people oriented" person
   - Develop trust and confidence in your staff
   - Mentor subordinates

2. *Sixth Sense*

   - Anticipate

- Become thoroughly familiar with your subject
- Think proactively
- Go with your "gut" feeling more often

3. *Leadership*

- Lead by example
- Providing leadership is not a part time job
- Empowerment of others needs even stronger leadership
- Leaders have many defining characteristics
- Leadership starts at the top; and, you are the top of whatever organizational unit it is that you are managing

4. *Options and Decision Making*

- Look at all your options before making a decision
- The easiest solution may not be the best solution
- You cannot "guarantee" the best solution

5. *Communicating-Relating-Waiting*

- Communicate in a clear, concise, and timely manner
- Develop both oral and written communication skills
- Communication goes vertically, horizontally and diagonally in any organization

6. *Risk Taking*

- A more effective manger is a risk taker
- Risk takers tend to be more open minded, better listeners, self-starters and have more self-confidence in themselves
- Only a person who risks is free

7. *Solution to Every Problem-Persistency*

- Be determined and persistent
- Offer solutions that may be viewed as unpopular

8. *Feedback; Positive and Negative*

  - Listen to all feedback
  - Negative feedback may lead to a source of a larger problem
  - Positive feedback gives us confidence
  - Solicit feedback
  - Do not be afraid of negative feedback

9. *Taking a Real Interest in Subordinates*

  - Show an interest in his/her work
  - Maintain interest
  - Listen to what subordinates have to say
  - Subordinates are also your customers

10. *If It Ain't Broke, Don't Fix It*

  - Don't make change solely for the sake of change
  - Always look for ways to improve things
  - Change is going to cost something
  - Change must make a difference in a positive way

11. *Developing Subordinates*

  - Look at all available tools to develop subordinates
  - A more intelligent and informed work force should lead to a better operation and employee morale
  - How you utilize a deputy or assistant is important
  - Get involved in the hiring process and select your team players if possible

12. *Micromanaging*

  - Micromanaging stifles creativity
  - Keep the decision making process at the lowest level possible
  - You can delegate authority, but you cannot delegate responsibility
  - Do not delegate and disengage

- Smaller organizations and organizational units are more likely to fall prey to micromanaging

13. *Is Everything Important?*

- Recognize that everything that you do is important, but some things are more important than others
- Prioritize work
- Be careful not to spend 80 percent of your time on 10 percent of your problems

14. *The Learning Process*

- Never stops
- Learn from everyone; supervisors, subordinates and customers
- You are not only a mentor/teacher, but a student as well
- Avoid the reputation as a "know it all"

15. *Focus, Focus, Focus*

- Screen out the unessential
- Maintain the big picture in mind
- Avoid developing "tunnel vision" solutions to problems

16. *Tuning Out to Tune In*

- Not only hear what is said but *listen* to what is being said
- Active listening is what this is all about
- Block out physical distractions

17. *Rocking the Boat*

- Do not be afraid to challenge higher management or organizational decisions that affect your unit
- Could lead to a paradigm shift in the way the organization conducts business
- Be ready to stand up to your convictions and if you "rock the boat" be prepared for the possibility that you may fall in the water

18. *Interaction and Interpersonal Skills*

- You are always interacting with someone
- Remember to put the "personal" into personnel
- You cannot isolate yourself in the work environment
- Continually hone your interpersonal skills

19. *A "Team Player", Not a "Yes Man"*

- The team concept is nothing new
- Recognize your role on the team and your contributions as an individual to the team efforts
- Understand that there are teams within teams
- Minimize the use of "my" when referring to employees or groups of employees: i.e. "my" secretary, "my" motor pool, etcetera.

20. *Goal Setting*

- Aim high but set realistic goals
- Do not set goals too low
- Start with the end in mind
- Goals and objectives may not be reached all of the time

21. *Facilitating and Controlling the Situation*

- There may be multiple factors to control, all at the same time
- Learn to facilitate
- Set clear agendas
- Do not be afraid to say "no"

22. *Use of Time*

- Make good use of your time, your subordinate's time and your customer's time
- Making good use of time is a personal matter
- Time is money

23. *It May Not Be Right, but that's the Way It Is—Most of the Time*

- Loyalty to an individual or to the organization is the key to understanding this concept
- Challenging or supporting organizational decisions can test your sense of loyalty

24. *Common Sense*

- Is sound and prudent but often unsophisticated judgment
- We all have it
- Always look for ways to get the job done, including use of common sense

25. *Responding*

- Respond to all questions and queries in a timely manner
- Provide correct answers
- Defer responses if need be
- Look at various types of responses; for example face-to-face, telephonic, written, etcetera.

26. *Believing That You Can Do Something*

- Believe in yourself
- Believe rather than *think* that you can make a difference
- Don't let a belief become an obsession

27. *Sexual Harassment in the Work Environment*

- Keep sex out of the work environment
- There are no winners in sexual harassment cases

28. *Work Windows*

- Develop a time-frame to get things done
- Make effective use of time management and workload distribution
- Avoid setting dead-lines

29. *Brainstorming*

- We practice the art of brainstorming almost daily
- Selection of the brainstorming participants is important
- Try to stay focused on the issue that you are brainstorming

30. *The WHAT IF Syndrome*

- More often than not the connotation of "if" is that we are not satisfied with what we did or the way that things turned out
- Do not *dwell* on the word "if'"
- Develop a "Lessons learned" attitude when trying to answer the question "What *if* we did this, or that?"

31. *Evaluating*

- Evaluate your own performance and the performance of individuals and teams
- Try to base performance on the "Whole Man" concept
- Be objective and firm, but fair in your evaluations
- To improve performance you must be able to evaluate performance—Consider results in your evaluations

32. *Staying Calm, Cool and Collected*

- Keep yourself under control
- Think with your head at all times
- The customer is not always right

33. *A Goof Day and Inner Peace*

- Your peace of mind is important
- Indulge yourself in a passion that fuels your deepest inner calm
- Leave your work at the workplace when you depart for home or to the local pub

34. *Nice Going!*

- The three most important things that keep employees happy and dedicated are job stability, recognition and compensation
- Reward people

35. *That "Half Step" to the Rear*

- Gives you the time to re-evaluate, to reassess or to pause and reflect on whatever you are doing
- Indicates patience with yourself and with those involved in the activity that you are managing
- It does not indicate that you are backing away from something or afraid to make a decision

36. *Room for Improvement*

- There is always room for improvement
- You may have to "reengineer"
- Improvements should lead to more efficient operations and make your managing less complicated
- Think outside of the box

37. *Underestimating Yourself*

- Never underestimate yourself
- Subordinates are looking to you for direction
- Work up to your potential and understand that there is nothing wrong with not being on a fast track

38. *Giving Yourself Credit*

- Don't be reluctant or afraid to pat yourself on the back
- This is not going against the "we" not "me" principle
- If you get a chance to write your own performance appraisal, go for it

39. *"I Don't Know"*

- No one knows it all
- Finding answers helps you identify resources

40. *The Six P's*

- Prior Planning Prevents Piss Poor Performance
- Plan ahead
- Keep in mind that planning is one thing, implementing is another
- Do first things first
- KISS it: Keep It Simple Sweetheart

41. *Strengths and Weaknesses*

- Recognize that we all have strengths and weaknesses
- Work on improving your limitations and weaknesses
- Be honest with yourself

42. *Being Consistent*

- Do not let exceptions become the rule
- Abuse of policy may lead to restrictions
- Exceptions may have an adverse effect on employee morale

43. *The Means May Not Always Justify the End*

- It's not where you start, it's where you finish
- There has to be some balance between the means and the end
- Focusing only on end results may not be in the best interests of the organization

44. *Jumping to Conclusions*

- Gather as much information as possible before making decisions
- Incorporate a 360 degree concept in decision making
- If you are in a position that requires an interpretation of personnel policy; lean towards an interpretation that favors the employee

45. *Making Everyone Happy, All of the Time*

- You cannot make everyone happy all of the time
- Be as accommodating as possible
- Treat people in a reasonable and fair manner
- The customer may not always be right, but he/she are still your customer

46. *Looking Back*

- You can't bring back the past but you can learn from it
- Don't cling to how things were done in the past

47. *Passing the Buck*

- Do not look for a scapegoat or try to pass the blame
- We should all be held accountable for our actions
- Incorporate the concept of TQM or shared responsibility and that everyone is a shareholder in the unit that you manage

48. *Assumptions*

- Balance assumption with hard evidence
- To assume may make an ASS of U and ME

49. *Go for It*

- Implement in a controlled but decisive and timely manner
- Have determination to carry things through
- Take one step at a time and continue to evaluate feedback
- Do not procrastinate

50. *Networking*

- Networking is a 360 degree activity
- Use all media tools to network
- Networking helps in career development
- Networking will help you learn from others

51. *Attitude*

- A positive attitude will help turn negatives into positives
- Never get down on yourself
- A positive attitude will keep you a "winner" and not turn you into a "whiner"
- A positive attitude is contagious

52. *Doing What Ya Gotta Do*

- Some of the things that you do in the work environment may not be popular
- Managers are not always nice guys
- Always look for windows of opportunity
- May lead to a career change

53. *Strokin'*

- You may not always be in a position that allows you to tell it like it is
- Knowing your customer will help you hone this skill
- Public Relations is a mix of fact and Strokin'

54. *A Sense of Humor*

- Helps shorten those long ten and twelve hour days
- Lowers stress in the work environment
- Plays a role in the way that we communicate with others

55. *Questioning*

- Question supervisors, subordinates, co-workers and customers
- Educates everyone
- Is an avenue to enhance our situational awareness
- An informed manager is a more effective manager
- Seek and ye shall find

56. *Order in Your Disorder*

- There is not magic formula for organizing ones' self
- Organizing yourself will allow you to make better use of your time
- Incorporate both time and space management in the equation

APPENDIX B

UNDP Country Classifications

High Human Development Countries	*Medium Human Development Countries*	*Low Human Development Countries*
Antiqua and Barbuda	Albania	Angola
Argentina	Algeria	Benin
Australia	Armenia	Burkina Faso
Austria	Azerbijan	Burundi
Bahamas	Bangladesh	Central African Republic
Bahrain	Belarus	Chad
Barbados	Belize	Congo
Belgium	Bhutan	Congo, Dem. Rep. of the
Brunei Darussalam	Bolivia	Cote d'Ivoire
Canada	Bosnia and Herzegovina	Djibouti
Chile	Botswana	Eritrea
Costa Rica	Brazil	Ethiopia
Croatia	Bulgaria	Gambia
Cuba	Cambodia	Guinea

Cypress	Cameroon	Guinea-Bissau
Czech Republic	Cape Verde	Haiti
Denmark	China	Kenya
Estonia	Columbia	Lesotho
Finland	Comoros	Madagascar
France	Dominica	Malawi
Germany	Dominican Republic	Mali
Greece	Ecuador	Mauritania
Hong Kong, China (SAR)	Egypt	Mozambique
Hungary	El Salvador	Niger
Iceland	Equatorial Guinea	Nigeria
Ireland	Fiji	Pakistan
Israel	Gabon	Rwanda
Italy	Georgia	Senegal
Japan	Ghana	Sierra Leone
Korea, Republic of	Grenada	Tanzania, U. Rep. of
Kuwait	Guatemala	Timor-Leste
Latvia	Guyana	Togo
Lithuania	Honduras	Uganda
Luxembourg	India	Yemen
Malta	Indonesia	Zambia
Mexico	Iran, Islamic Rep. of	Zimbabwe
Netherlands	Jamaica	*(36 countries/areas)*

High Human Development

New Zealand
Norway
Poland

Medium Human Development

Jordan
Kazakhstan
Kyrgzstan

Portugal
Qatar
Saint Kits and Nevis
Seychelles
Singapore
Slovakia
Slovenia
Spain
Sweden
Switzerland
Trinidad and Tobago
United Arab Emirates
United Kingdom
United States
Uruguay
(55 countries/areas)

Lao People's Dem. Rep.
Lebanon
Libyan Arab Jamahiriya
Macedonia, TFYR
Malaysia
Maldives
Mauritius
Moldova, Rep. of
Mongolia
Morocco
Myanmar
Namibia
Nepal
Nicaragua
Occupied Palestinian Territories
Oman
Panama
Papua New Guinea
Paraguay
Peru
Philippines
Romania
Russian Federation
Saint Lucia
St. Vincent & the Grenadines
Samoa (Western)
Sao Tome and Principe
Saudi Arabia
Solomon Islands
South Africa
Sri Lanka
Sudan
Suriname
Swaziland
Syrian Arab Republic
Tajikistan
Thailand
Tonga

Medium Human Development

Tunisia
Turkey
Turkmenistan
Ukraine
Uzbekistan
Vanuatu
Venezuela
Viet Nam
(86 countries/areas)

Recapitulation

High Human Development	55 countries/areas
Medium Human Development	86 countries/areas
Low Human Development	36 countries/areas
Countries/areas where data is not computed	17 countries/areas
	==============
Total	194 countries/areas

APPENDIX C

———◆———

74 Risks Identified in Author's Thesis

Internal Risk

1. Loss of company technology if imported into Bolivia.
2. Direct company involvement in illegal business practices.
3. Alienation of ex-patriot employees because of poor working conditions in host country or inadequate company incentives or benefits.
4. Selection of wrong foreign partner if a joint venture is undertaken.
5. Acts of terrorism on personnel or plant.
6. Loss of face in industry if the venture fails.
7. Company lack of understanding of host country problems.
8. Not adjusting to host country cultural differences.
9. Generating conflict within the parent company.
10. Loss of control of foreign operations to the home office.
11. Overstocking of inventories.
12. Poor communication facilities.
13. Logistical problems stemming from inadequate transportation systems.
14. Not obtaining knowledge of local market prior to starting operations.
15. Weather.
16. Development of a "negative attitude" towards Bolivia after the operation has been set up and is functioning.
17. Poor quality of locally produced products or non-availability of local materials such as cement

18. Short "tourist" season.
19. Home country regulation.
20. Accusation of human rights violations.
21. Selection of wrong management structure.
22. Too rapid growth of company in the foreign environment.
23. Geological problems, primarily in the petroleum sector.
24. Inadequate expatriate staffing within host country to draw from.

Financial Risks

1. Stability of host country currency.
2. Cost of host country currency.
3. Floating rates of currency exchange.
4. Devaluation.
5. Host country inflation.
6. Foreign capital availability for re-exportation.
7. Host country financial policies.
8. Host country taxation; both internal and pertaining to foreign companies.
9. Black market foreign currency exchange.
10. One sided economy based on export of on-renewable resources.
11. Underdeveloped capital and financial markets.
12. Multiple currencies.

Social Risks

1. Labor union influence.
2. Accusation of company insensitivity to host country needs.
3. Host country general attitudes towards foreign companies.
4. Finding adequate local staffing.
5. Accusation of discriminatory hiring/firing policies towards local employees.
6. Lack of communication because of language.
7. Wide-spread corruption and lack of moral integrity in both the public and private sectors.
8. Strikes or work stoppages based on non-work related reasons; for example, support of other unions.

9. Local takeover of operations by workers or local populace as opposed to government nationalization.
10. Non-availability of competent advisors.
11. High frequency of petty thievery.
12. Competition from contraband activities.
13. Social revolution or uprising in host country.

Political Risks

1. Nationalization of the company.
2. Accusation of involvement in host country political/economic decisions.
3. Host country regulation.
4. Uncertainty of host country foreign policies.
5. Host country government stability.
6. Host government future restraints on operations once the venture becomes successful.
7. Unfair competition from host country competitors.
8. Host government discrimination between foreign and local companies.
9. Instigating or causing government to government confrontations.
10. Political immaturity in Bolivia.
11. Bureaucratic red-tape and interference including customs delays in retrieving imported goods and materials.
12. Unilateral government interpretations of laws, policy or contractual agreements.
13. Non-fulfillment by the government of contractual agreements.
14. Retroactive government decrees primarily in areas of worker related issues such as wage increases.
15. Andean Pact restrictions.
16. Inconsistency in interpretations of policy within the same government agency or between government agencies.
17. Influence of outside agencies such as the IMF on internal Bolivian matters.
18. Lack of continuity between different elected governments.
19. Host country environmental controls.
20. Foreign trade barriers.

21. Unfavorable settlement of judicial disputes, normally against the foreign company.
22. Arrest of company officials.
23. Host country in-country travel restrictions.
24. Inconsistency in host country government planning.
25. Limited infra-structure in host country.